Images of War
Sherman Tank

RARE PHOTOGRAPHS FROM WARTIME ARCHIVES

Gavin Birch

Pen & Sword
MILITARY

First published in Great Britain in 2005 by
PEN & SWORD MILITARY
an imprint of
Pen & Sword Books Ltd,
47 Church Street, Barnsley,
South Yorkshire.
S70 2AS

ISBN 1-84415-187-5

A CIP catalogue record for this book is available from the
British Library

Printed and bound in Great Britain by CPI UK

Pen & Sword Books Ltd incorporates the imprints of
Pen & Sword Aviation, Pen & Sword Maritime,
Pen & Sword Military, Pen & Sword Select, Pen & Sword
Military Classics, Leo Cooper, Wharncliffe Local History,

For a complete list of Pen & Sword titles please contact:
PEN & SWORD BOOKS LIMITED
47 Church Street, Barnsley, South Yorkshire, S70 2AS, England.
E-mail: enquiries@pen-and-sword.co.uk
Website: www.pen-and-sword.co.uk

Contents

Acknowledgements 4

Foreword 6

Source of Photographs
    British and American Focus 10

Chapter One
    'AFPOO' – The War on Film 11

Chapter Two
    The Sherman Story – Design and Development 15

Chapter Three
    The UK Home Army – First UK Sherman to the 'Funny' 21

Chapter Four
    North Africa – British Action – Egypt, Libya, Tunisia 49

Chapter Five
    The Mediterranean – Sicily and the Hop to Italy 63

Chapter Six
    NW Europe – Normandy to Belgium & Holland 81

Chapter Seven
    NW Europe – Spring 1945 into Germany and Victory 105

Chapter Eight
    The Far East – British Shermans up the Jungle 123

Chapter Nine
    US Shermans – Wartime American Action 141

Chapter Ten
    Model List – Identifying Sherman Variants 169

Acknowledgements

In 1944 my grand father, Frank Birch, was a British citizen soldier. He left his job on pre-war South London Bus routes with colleagues from London Transport when their entire depot was called up to the Royal Army Service Corps (RASC) during WW2. Of his many assignments with the British Army in Europe he spent most of his time driving Scammel Pioneer bridging trucks. From the French coast through Holland toward Germany, he built the bridges that allowed the armour spearheads to advance. He died when I was a child, but not before engendering a lasting impression with his photographs and real life experience of the war in North West Europe during 1944-45. This photo is fundamentally identical to the many portraits of our relatives I have seen on the living room mantle-pieces of my friends over the years. Our fathers and grandfathers, and now great grandfathers - those generations who downed tools in civilian life to pick up the tools for Victory. His wartime 'snaps' began a fascination with the photography of the period. The stories relayed to me as a child were full of conscript humour, but edged with a certain pathos, a sense of witnessing history in the knowledge he was playing a minute part in it all. His humorous recollections were partnered by tales of great tragedy, especially when recalling the columns of DP's (Displaced Persons) he saw strafed by enemy aircraft at the roadside. Perhaps a child should not have been told of such things but the effect was to make his war stories REAL.

He gave me an appreciation of an entirely different age, a period in history which will continue to capture my imagination and that I will always continue to try to comprehend.

I also thank: Brigadier Henry Wilson and the team at Pen & Sword Books Limited for their support and fruitful suggestions throughout the project. Hilary Roberts and the staff at the Photographic Archive, IWM, & BCMH members Mr Chris McCarthy, Mr Mike Taylor, and Mr Alan Jeffreys for historical and compilation advice. Friend and fellow graduate Mr Paul Billington for accompanying me on a research trip to the Ardennes region of Belgium in 2003 where we spent many fascinating days covering the ground on which the Battle of The Bulge was fought, and for our investigation of the Remagen Bridgehead during the Sixtieth Anniversary of its capture in March, 2005 - it's simply imperative to see the lay of the land when trying to understand how a battle played out. I also acknowledge the private owners around the world who have endeavoured to save and exhibit many original Sherman Tanks in running form. It is through their commendable efforts that the generations of tomorrow will not only view photographs like these, but will hear, smell and touch something tangible of the experience of crewing the Sherman Tank in wartime. Finally, I thank Vicky.

Gavin Birch (c) 2005

Foreword

Authors of military books often make the claim of using rare unpublished photographs in publications but frequently I have been disappointed by their photographic content. They often use either blurred images, photographs digitally enhanced, or originals cropped or reversed from older books. In endeavouring to compile THE SHERMAN TANK I have returned to primary source negatives held under Crown Copyright regulation by the Imperial War Museum. To undertake a project such as this, one has to bare certain concessions in mind from the outset. There are sequences of photographs in circulation which anyone who has taken a passing interest in the Sherman Tank will instantly recognise - These are reprinted consistently. Sometimes they are incorrectly dated, identified and even located. I have seen photos taken in Italy described as originating in Burma! I have elected to reject these shots for this publication as they are overused and thus have become instantly recognisable and a little tired. Great photographs in their own right no question, but a little tired. You, like me, want something new and this book offers that. Over eighty per cent of these photographs have never appeared in previous publications before, and those that have, are included to give an accurate date, caption, or reference number.

There also exists the notion that every battle and every constituent part of these battles was captured on film as we have become accustomed to viewing WW2 in black and white and that therefore a new book on the Sherman Tank will have fully comprehensive detailed photography of every single design change made to this tank in war years. This is simply not the case in this book and for solid reasons. The cameramen responsible for the photographs in this book were working under orders and to an agenda in extremely difficult circumstances, (See Chapter 1 - The AFPU). Thus one cannot expect perfect 360 degree cataloguing shots of how each variant and model differed. During many actions along the frontline the cameramen were not present in that sector, perhaps having been given a more mundane assignment on that particular day. In many actions the nature of the fighting was so ferocious that the combat conditions made the taking of photographs impossible. In some cases the angle from which the tank has been photographed defies a definitive identification as interchangeable parts were used. The aim for this publication is to provide a genuine panoramic illustration of the Sherman Tank in its many guises as demonstrated by the official photography of the period. It is not a technical manual, appraisal of the machinery or guide to making scale models of the tank although will be helpful in all of those applications. The photographs in this book will certainly inspire some new scale model dioramas for sure, but those publications already exist, and now even original US Ordnance Manuals have been reprinted and are available to those restoring and rebuilding the real thing.

I would argue that the Sherman is the most recognisable tank of all time, and certainly of armour types that saw action in the 1939-45 war. 'Sherman M4 Tank' is of course an amalgamation of official nomenclature, and nickname that adhered when the tank was pressed into service. Recent debate has even asked if wartime crew referred to their tanks as Shermans, for surely they were Medium M4's as the covers of original tech manuals refer to them? Initially for the American producers of the tank, and US Army intended users, it was only known as 'Tank, M4, Medium'. The British referred to this new armour type as the 'General Sherman' and then 'Sherman Tank' in compliance with their policy of naming American armour in British Service after US Civil War Generals such as Jeb 'Stuart', 'Grant' and 'Lee.' Within a short period all troops knew the tank as the Sherman, and Sherman M4 in official parlance, and only rarely described themselves as belonging to a 'Medium Tank' unit.

It was manufactured in huge numbers with production figures exceeding the totals of all German types of armour combined in wartime production. They saw service on almost every battlefront in every campaign and were used by Russian, British, American, French, Polish, Indian, New Zealand, Canadian and Chinese armoured forces on the Allied team. Only a handful were sent to Australia for testing and one or two of these examples survived into museum captivity down under. Even the Germans 're-badged' a captured few (German Shermans) over the last months of the war. So many were produced during 1941-45 that they can still be discovered in locations around the world from gate guardians, to privately owned vintage vehicle showstoppers, on firing ranges and in museum displays. Sherman Tanks have frequently been used as contemporary monuments on the wartime battlefields too. Perhaps you are familiar with some that you have viewed while taking a holiday? Examples can be viewed at Montormel in Normandy, the town square in Bastogne, in fact all over the Ardennes and at Slapton Sands in Devon to name a handful of locations. The late Ken Small orchestrated recovery of the Devon Sherman in the UK from out at sea to where it now stands in memoriam on the promenade. It had been lost in the US pre-invasion training exercise called TIGER during Spring, 1944 and is now visited by thousands of holiday-makers each year.

As recently as January, 2004 a story appeared via the Internet about a wartime Sherman M4A3 105mm (HVSS) Tank being captured and restored during the Iraq War (2003) by the 1st Brigade Combat Team, 4th US Infantry Division at Camp Raider within Iraq. I spoke with the command team from 4th US Infantry Division who relayed the story in preparation of this book. The vehicle was found at an abandoned Iraqi armoured vehicle school along a main highway. By the order of Colonel James Hickey, CO 1st BCT, 4th Infantry Division the Sherman was loaded

The Sherman used as a monument, which stands in McAuliffe Square, Bastogne as memorial to the seige of December 1944 during the Battle of The Bulge. The paint is worn away from the hands of the inquisitive around an impact point created by a shell that knocked it out down the right side of the hull. This tank had six victories by the time it reached the hamlet of Renaument during December, 1944. There it became stuck in boggy ground and thus an easy target. Today it creates a focal point in the square. (March, 2003.)

onto a heavy equipment transport trailer and taken to Forward Operating Base 'Raider'. Colonel Hickey also commanded the unit which eventually came to surround and capture Saddam Hussein in the now famous 'hideaway hole.' At Camp Raider it was restored by mechanics and specialists from the 4th Forward Support Battalion, although it had been in relatively good condition when discovered. It is armed with a 105mm Howitzer as main armament, with .30 calibre machine-gun and a .50 anti-aircraft heavy machine gun on the turret. It is likely that this example of the Sherman will find it's way to the museum at Fort Hood, Texas. Probably captured from Iran during Iraq's war in the 1970s, the Sherman will remain a preserved exhibit for the rest of its days.

So if Sherman tanks are easily recognisable, and so abundant in museum collections and at private displays then why is another book required covering this theme? There are many reasons: Not least because photo reference books go out of print, and those published in the late 60's and 70's are increasingly expensive and difficult to find on the subject. Quality has much improved in the process of transferring photo to page and those early books demonstrate a range of photo reproduction standards. The photographic illustrations in this book are largely unpublished and have remained in the archives, thumbed through only a few times since the end of the Second World War. For that reason alone it is bringing new primary source evidence to the table for contemporary generations. The photographs are artistically composed strong images and were taken by professional cameramen as opposed to the often blurred imagery of the enlisted amateur photographer. Some are what I would term reaction snaps, taken either in combat or with instinctive notions that the lense was about to capture a shot that could be used to illustrate an important story. They provide honest and detailed testament to how these tanks were used, appeared, and indeed faired in combat. Often museum examples such as the Sherman M4A4 exhibited at the Imperial War Museum in London are only representative of the bare bones of the vehicle. While the IWM example is fairly complete, much has gone missing from it's original wartime appearance over the sixty odd years since it was in service. I have been involved with the repaint of this particular vehicle and refitting of some external original fittings during 2004. However, the tank's engine bay is barren. The A57 Chrysler Multibank engine resides in an impressive rebuilt state exhibited seperately at the IWM's Duxford site at the entrance to The Land Warfare Hall. Observe the original photography featured in this book and you will see that the Sherman in service came to life with stored equipment, crew adaptations, vehicle naming, and camouflage paint schemes plus a range of unit identification markings. Every one is different despite the significant mass production figures.

Finally, I still consider the quality of these prints to be second to none even though I have now been studying them for some time. Sixty odd years on from when first taken, they have all been hand printed from original negative, and for the first time the military veteran, enthusiast, vehicle restorer, and modeller will gain a selection of crystal clear images that take one back in an instant to the moment the shutter operated within the camera. I feel this book offers invaluable primary source material, and thus it was imperative to endeavour to bring this remarkable selection of images together for the attention of a wider audience. All photographs are referenced with an IWM catalogue number in this publication making the process of ordering your own prints easier than ever from the IWM archive.

Source of Photographs
British and American Focus

A The photographs you are about to view have all been discovered through extensive research by the author at the Photographic Archive of London's Imperial War Museum. Licenses have been sought and granted to the author for all photographs, they remain CROWN COPYRIGHT.

I feel it is important to note that in my view the archive is greatly under valued and indeed under-used. It exists for the Public as well as for the professional historian. Anyone can request to view the albums kept there by appointment, and can order prints, essential in modelling and restoration guidance. Containing in excess of eight million photographic images, it holds an enormously rich source of material on the Two World Wars but its coverage spans the entire twentieth century and is international in scope. The photographs I have chosen for this publication only scratch the surface of the amazing variety of subject matter recorded.

It is a truly unique record of conflict. The photos featured in this publication are mainly of British Army subject matter and this is simply due to the abundance of AFPU material in the collection compared with that of American or Commonwealth origin. The American material was discovered in the US Embassy Collection which the museum also holds. These are photographs taken by assorted agency photographers and the US Signal Corps covering all aspects of the Second World War from an American perspective - therefore they have warranted their own unique chapter in this publication. Originally they were part of the Library of the United States Information Service based at the US Embassy in London, but were transferred to the Imperial War Museum on 10 November, 1947. Neither the print nor negative runs are complete in the US Embassy Collection and prints are filed under subject classification so can be frustrating to search through. Caption detail is also well below the standard of the British Official prints.

Photographic Archive, Imperial War Museum, Lambeth Road, London, SE1 6HZ
Tel: +44 (0) 0207 416 5338 • Fax: +44 (0) 0207 416 5355,
Email: photos@iwm.org.uk • website: www.iwm.org.uk

(Blemishes on the photographs are due either to the wartime censor obliterating unit markings on vehicles and uniforms, or in some cases is due to the rarity of the subject matter being deemed significant enough to use a sub standard print in order to illustrate a point. These blemished prints have been kept to a minimum.)

Chapter One

'AFPOO'
The War on Film

The images you may have viewed of the British Army during the Second World War in a range of magazines, original newspapers and new books originated most probably from the work of the AFPU and yet little is widely known about how they worked and indeed who they were. Most of the images presented in *this* publication also originate from the work of the Army Film and Photographic Unit and the others have come via the US Information Service when based at the US Embassy in London. So, before advancing any further in our consideration of the Sherman M4 Tank it is appropriate to consider the work of the cameramen briefly. The cinematographers and stills cameramen, many of whom gave their lives in efforts to record the war both as a diary for the army but also for us, are certainly owed due credit.

No.1 Army Film and Photographic (AFPU) was formed in London during 1941 as the Sherman design was being developed in North America and put into production. It originally consisted of twenty-six Sergeant cameramen, both still and movie, under the control of Major David Macdonald. Recruited to create a unit with a common aim, these men had responded to calls for troops with experience of the film industry or still photography in a professional capacity. They were given only two objectives – to record The Desert War for newsreels and press, and to create images for official army records. Shipped to Cairo in November of 1941 they were attached to the 8th Army in preparation for filming the desert campaign. After a delay due to their camera equipment being lost at sea when the ship transporting it was sunk, replacement De Vry and Eyemo cameras caught up with them. Their cameras were not the best available, and to capture some of the shots in this book cameramen had to position themselves in highly exposed positions. With no telephoto lens equivalents, they indeed had to be in the action, to get the photograph. Next they began to attach themselves to the various fighting units in the desert. Many problems hindered first efforts, not least the desert conditions. No transport had been allocated to the AFPU, therefore the cameramen would have to hitch rides with the fighting troops. This created initial animosity toward them as only being armed with camera and spare film some jealousy was felt by the combat troops. The reaction the first cameramen probably received was something like *'Ain'tcha got a rifle then mate?'*

The one positive environmental element in their favour was the superb lighting which the desert sun provided on clear dry days. You will appreciate this from the North African and Mediterranean series of photographs you view some sixty years on. Coverage they achieved was limited by their lack of transport, and therefore much early footage only captured air attacks at distance. Little early wartime photography showed an enemy at a personal range. After the Afrika Korps pushed the 8th Army back to El Alamein, recapturing Tobruk on the way, the Army Film Unit was reassigned to 8th Army HQ. Understanding of the AFPU's work increased with growing recognition, and the unit was seen as a more valuable asset for morale than at first thought. With the direction of the war about to reverse the encouragement of Home Front morale was something to be protected. This helped facilitate better access to the battlefield for the AFPU men, brought acceptance and further expansion. From that point on cameramen were teamed with stills photographers, two to a jeep and let free to chase their story. Something only the freelance journalists can hope for under modern battlefield conditions today. AFPU jeep teams based with 8th Army HQ could roam at will rather than be attached to a single assigned battalion. The resulting footage from these forays appeared in the films *'Desert Victory'* and *'Tunisian Victory'* plus hundreds of still photographs, a handful of which are featured in this book.

In recent years it has been the fashion to focus only on the small collection of footage from the North African campaign which is known to have been faked by pressmen associated with the AFPU. I must emphasise that recent research has shown this was a minute amount compared with the bulk of their work. The majority of cameramen worked professionally under conditions of extreme danger – AFPU members were killed accompanying a Commando raid on Tobruk, and many were captured as their forward positions were overrun in all campaigns. Of the initial 26 members of No.1 AFPU: Four cameramen were killed, five wounded and four taken prisoner leaving just 13 cameramen and a tally sheet showing fifty per cent losses.

After the fall of Tunis, No.1 and No.2 AFPUs joined together. No.2 had followed the Americans through the campaign while No1 had been attached to the 8th Army. The amalgamation of the two groups, with new replacement staff allowed the concentrated effort of much greater coverage and was just in time for the invasion of Sicily in 1943. Preparations took place in Tripoli and they later covered the beach assaults, Cassino battles and the drive to Naples and onto Rome. AFPU Officer Alan Whicker beat General Mark Clark into Rome and was there, waiting, to capture his entry into the city. Further teams were being assembled in the UK in readiness for the assault on Northwest Europe and much of the well recognised Normandy invasion film footage and photography stems from the work of expanded AFPU units. By 1944, the AFPU had become an accepted part of how British war reporting was taking place. No. 5 AFPU Section was set up especially to cover the Normandy Campaign. Anywhere between a dozen and two dozen stills cameramen would be in the field at any one time. Images they captured on film would be sent to the War Office for censorship and then to the Ministry of Information (MOI) Photographs Division for additional vetting and further distribution if passed. The amphibious landings in Normandy promised incredible opportunities for these photographers, and they rarely missed them in capturing the emotion and look of the campaign that followed. It was AFPU Sgt Photographer Mapham who sprinted ashore on Queen sector of Sword Beach to make history with one famous photograph: an image that again crossed the globe during the 60th Anniversary of D-Day in June 2004. Turning at the top of the beach, he raised his Super Ikonta camera and focussed on a scene which captured men of the 13/18th Hussars helping wounded comrades ashore through the early morning mist and smoke from the bombardment of the shoreline.

BUT WHY NO COLOUR PHOTOGRAPHS?

Colour film stock was a total rarity in Britain for most of the Second World War years but miniscule amounts were available for official purposes from mid-war. Small amounts were also privately purchased from outlets when on leave overseas or from wealthy American officers who were having Kodak stock shipped from the States. During the NW Europe campaign it was hardly ever available, and certainly not to the AFPU Sergeant photographers. The officers who did manage to inherit colour stock retained it for special occasions such as celebrations, ceremonial parades, portraits or off duty poses. Consider the books you have purchased on the war and you will see little has ever found its way into the public domain. Another reason for not using colour film was that a market for the finished product did not exist at home in wartime Britain nor with publications elsewhere in the Commonwealth. There was very limited opportunity for magazines and papers to reproduce colour prints back on the mainland. Severe restrictions had been placed upon the National Press in order to save inks, but the greater purpose was to impress upon the public the air of wartime austerity and gravitas. In the tradition of the wartime slogan 'Make Do and Mend' – It was black and white photography only for the duration!

ORDERS FOR CAMERA MEN ON THE BATTLEFIELD

The photographers of AFPU were encouraged to compose photo-stories in their official guidelines produced by the MOI (Ministry of Information). 'Sergeant Photographer... This Is Your Job' (1942) listed the publicity and propaganda purposes of official British photography. It focussed upon topical news stories, the importance of selecting 'the sturdiest, toughest types' as subjects, but also pleaded that 'cheery stuff' could be overdone. It closed with the warning: '*You must go out to treat subjects seriously!*' Onward through the liberation of Paris, the crossing of the Belgian-Dutch border on 21 September, 1944 and the liberation of Brussels. The AFPU men continued recording the progress of the campaign in NW Europe as they were doing in Italy. They relentlessly filmed the Airborne assaults mid 1944, XXX Corps' efforts to reach Arnhem and events in the Ardennes, the snow covered mountain battles in Italy. The natural barrier of the Rhine river in NW Europe saw them preparing for the Rhine Crossing operation to take place on 24 March 1945, but they could not yet envisage the sights that would greet them within the month on reaching Belsen Camp. The impact of the AFPU photographs taken at Belsen were also of enormous evidential significance.

During the NW European campaign these men took approximately 25,000 images alone which were distributed throughout Britain, her Allies and the rest of the world. Their work in North Africa, The Far East, Mediterranean and Europe offers us a unique account of the range of human experience of war. From the routine everyday duty to those monumental events that denote the way-points of history the AFPU legacy, and those of the freelance US photo-journalists has provided the backbone for this and many historical publications.

Take a moment to acknowledge and remember their efforts in recording a World War on film.

Chapter Two

The Sherman Story –
Design and Development

There were 15,153 75mm armed Sherman tanks alone, supplied to Britain by the end of 1944. The Sherman tank was one of the first armoured vehicles to be mass produced anywhere, and was designed over a relatively quick period due to urgent demand for armour of its type at the front in early war years. This demand simply originated from disastrous inter-war planning. American Industry had no experience of mass producing armoured tanks, and was also recovering from having survived the Depression just a decade earlier. America's isolationist stance contributed nothing to the urgency of re-equipping a modernized army for World War. The inter-war tank designers and military planners had failed to examine the three primary design features of firepower versus protection versus manoeuvrability in real depth and to settle on their armoured warfare doctrine in any great detail. American planners could not decide whether tanks would be fighting other tanks on the battlefields in a future war, or supporting foot soldiers. In Britain the inter-war tank designers had also been struggling with the new concept of fluid mobile armoured warfare. Should the tank fulfil a support role for the infantry, or should it become an instrument dealing the striking blow that secures the battlefront victory? Any visit to The Tank Museum at Bovington will demonstrate how confused British designers were in conceiving a worthwhile armoured fighting vehicle during the 1930s, especially after the Director of Mechanization in the UK ordered all development work to stop on a replacement for a British Medium Tank. Every experimental shape and size is exhibited, but not a single one that actually promised reliable results. Some experimental types bristle with inadequate light machine guns, some have small calibre main guns with limited traverse and elevation located in Flash Gordon inspired sponsons – laughable almost and disastrous!

Something that was so right by comparison however was a concept which began life in the USA during 1940 with the request to mount the proven US 75mm M3 Gun in a new turret, mounted on top of a fast armoured vehicle to fulfil a medium tank role. The first Shermans were in full production by late 1941. The Sherman was an unsophisticated piece of machinery making it easy to repair, cheap and quick to produce, but rugged due to the solid materials used in its construction. Its reliable chassis unit went on to provide the foundation for a huge range of specialized adaptations as well as its proven success as a turret tank. Main strengths stemmed from its simple construction which produced the conditions for it being simple to operate. Conscription of new citizen soldiers such as rural farm labour, factory and railroad workers meant that a proportion of this diverse range of men found themselves at tank schools wearing the uniform of the Armoured Division trooper here and in the US. The Axis advances across the world by 1942 ruled out years of expensive and professional training. Crews and tanks were needed instantly. Once round an open field and the trainee Sherman driver would have a basic grasp of the driving controls before further instruction continued. The crew tasks carried out at each station of the Sherman were designed with simple manual actions in mind, not only were the individual tasks straightforward, but the ability to learn the other crew members' responsibilities was thus possible, and often sensibly adopted in action in case of death or injury on the battlefield. Road wheels could be changed manually by the crew, and the track could also be removed for repair by the crew as illustrated in the Far East chapter of this book. When one considers Tiger or Panther track in size and weight comparison only heavy lifting equipment could assist the larger German armour in instances of repairing the running gear in the field.

The drawbacks from its urgent inception were also numerous and no historian denies the Sherman design arrived inclusive of many faults and weaknesses. Not least the thin armour chosen due to planning that the tank would be shipped overseas therefore weight reduction was a factor. Most overseas ports only had cranes capable of lifting a maximum load of forty tons, therefore a design of anything larger was deemed pointless. Inter-war doctrine added to the confusion, for the role of the Sherman was never clearly defined during its development. It was never envisaged in a tank against tank role initially, and therefore armour protection was listed as a lower priority. The mounting of large fuel tanks alongside the rear engine compartment, causing any escape of fuel from battle damage or loose connections on the hot engine to guarantee an inferno within seconds was also a flaw, as was its high silhouette due to the fitting of bulky radial engines. Thinner armour than German counterparts facilitated speed from a range of diesel and petrol powered engines, but at the cost of crew and ammunition protection. Production lines continued to complete tank after tank in their thousands, as more manufacturers became involved in component provision for Sherman production. Swathes of farmland on the outskirts of Detroit, Michigan were turned into huge production facilities under the auspices of Chrysler Corporation Head, K T Keller, as it was in other mid-western states.

The facility in Michigan became known as The Detroit Tank Arsenal and it was this capacity for production that made the Sherman the right tool for contribution toward victory. High production figures imbued the tank with ultimate attritional battlefield power. During Operation GOODWOOD in Normandy some uninjured crews who lost their armour in action were able to walk back to the rear area and collect another tank to proceed with the advance. At the close of the operation some 450 tanks in British service had been lost, but the Allied Force was re-equipped and continued onward. German armour losses at the closing of the Falaise pocket by comparison were simply irreplaceable. By mid-war the Sherman was fighting on all fronts for the Allied cause. This book features locations from Mandalay to Munich. M4 variants continued to evolve with new suspension units, track design, new turret castings, larger main guns and experimental additional armour plating throughout the war years and with the many armies it has served with since the Second World War.

Returning to pre-war 1938 we should consider briefly the design and development phases, and the gearing up of American industrial might toward the mass production of the famous Sherman turret tank models illustrated in this book. A feature of production methods in wartime was the inclusion, re-use or adaptation of as many existing parts from other vehicles into new designs as was possible. One reason for this was the influx of women into the factories who had no technical apprenticeship training, and individual tasks were thus de-skilled generally and reduced to simplest form. Many women were trained to perform highly skilled engineering work, but to integrate the large numbers of new staff into the factories a gradual programme was devised beginning with de-skilling. If an already proven component off the shelf could be utilised, this cut manufacturing time even further. The realisation on both sides of the Atlantic that a world war was inevitable in the late 1930s enforced rapid preparation. The US Army had already acknowledged the worth of the M3 Light Tank which had been accepted into service in armoured reconnaissance roles but they still required a stronger version, a Medium tank.

The Rock Island Arsenal worked up a new model known as the T5 (Phase 1 design) in 1938 which used many of the M3 Light Tank's already available parts including its 37mm main gun. It also featured Vertical Volute Suspension (VVS) and a Continental Radial air-cooled engine producing 250 BHP. The design of the T5 allowed for a barbette and turret, the 37mm main gun housed in the turret, and four .30 Browning machine guns mounted singly into sponsons on each corner of the barbette. Additionally another two .30 Brownings protruded from a fixed position mounting in the hull front. The Rock Island Arsenal had definitely hit upon the basics for a good medium tank, but not in its current incarnation. The T5 was developed through several further phases that year, including test use of wider tracks, and a larger power plant. Its overall weight, thus strength, was increased until it metamorphasized into the Medium tank, M2 of 1939. Clearly a development on from the T5 tank, the M2 owed much to the lighter M3 Light tanks including its main armament of the standard 37mm gun. A finalized version called the Medium tank M2A1 with redesigned turret was adopted in 1940 and was deemed to be the new standardized medium tank for the US Army. Despite ongoing debate about the role for the new M2A1 the reality was that it was immediately obsolete. It had been known for a year or two previous that the German armoured forces were having 7.5cm (75mm) main guns fitted into their tanks. Largely ignoring this information, the US Army continued to rely on the 37mm gun as the main weapon of newly designed medium tanks intended to command the battlefield.

Rearmament and war-preparation issues came to a head in August 1940. News from France was both grim, and indeed of major concern for US Army planners. The 75mm German gun was ruling the battlefield in the German accelerated drive through Belgium, Holland and France during the charge for the coastline. Their advance across hundreds of miles was being measured in days and weeks and not in the months or years of The First World War. Decisions were needed urgently. The Chief of the newly formed Armoured Forces, US Army and planners from the Ordnance Department worked hard to formulate specifications for an improved medium tank capable of opposing German armour. The test results from the experimental T5 Tank development and the resulting M2 and M2A1's would prove most helpful in this planning. Specifications were soon drawn up: another new tank, but it required much thicker armour, needed to be fast, needed a bigger gun – the 75mm, and this gun needed excellent traverse and elevation ability – it simply could not be restricted in a sponson, mounted into a turret on top of the tank with full 360 degree rotation. However, on examining the experimental work carried out in the two years prior they immediately ran into a problem. Little to no development work had concentrated on mounting the heavier 75mm gun in a turret – most work had concentrated on increasing sponson armaments, the power from engines, and mounting of more machine guns or improving track strength.

The experiments that had been recorded involved mounting a 75mm Pack Howitzer into a prototype T5E2 medium tank (The T5 phase III of experimentation from 1938), but results only existed where the howitzer had been mounted in a modified sponson on the right side of the front of the tank. Urgency created by the advances in Europe dictated that it was these experimental efforts that must be further concentrated upon. There was no time to begin designing a turret from scratch to house the 75. Redesign occurred rapidly and the result was the M3 Medium Tank. It now weighed 31 tons, was armed with a 75mm M3 Main Gun in the sponson, and retained a 37mm M6 gun and .30 machine gun in a turret on top of the vehicle. Additional .30 machine guns were mounted in the hull front and also on the turret cupola. See IWM H 20919 which illustrates one of the first M3 Lee tanks to arrive in the UK. The pilot model M3 was ready in January of 1941 and the standardized production models reached troops toward the middle of 1941. Many were supplied both to Russia and to Britain as H20919 demonstrates.

Companies such as the Baldwin Locomotive Works, Pullman Standard Car Company, Lima Loco Works and The Pressed Steel Car Company all had British government contracts for the M3 Tank. British Tank Commission contracts asked for some slight alterations and the resulting production models were know as Grant Tanks. In Canada armoured forces were also looking to bulk up their strength with new armour so the Canadian government contracted with the Montreal Locomotive Works Division , part of The American Locomotive Corporation for the construction of some 1,157 tanks based on the M3 design also. It was the first Medium American tank to see action in the 1939-45 war both in Russia and Libya and feedback from crews was countenanced. Important standards were certainly set with the M3 such as the power-traversed turrets and gyrostabilizers for the guns which appeared again in the later Shermans. However, the feedback was not all positive. British Armoured Forces using Grants were in violent action at Gazala in Libya during May of 1942. Troops found that US planners back in August of 1940 had been absolutely correct in identifying the sponson mounted 75mm as a weakness. British crews found the limited traverse and elevation of the 75mm gun of the M3 and M3A1 Lee variants a huge disadvantage, often driving their vehicles toward their target in order to achieve a line of fire. The high silhouette overall of the tank in flat desert surroundings created a suicidal armoured vehicle to be caught in the open with. The gun was powerful however, and vastly improved up the 37mm still fitted in the turret, and there was relief that firepower disadvantage was at least diminishing.

Changes were incorporated into the design as stop gap measures more than serious attempts to placate crews. The original design of the M3 series had a riveted hull and used a Continental Wright R-975-EC2 or R-975 Petrol power plant. The M3A1 used a new cast hull in the hope of providing stronger protection for the crew and eliminating weak points where armour plate had been riveted together on the M3. The M3A2 was similar again but used a welded hull manufactured from individually cut armour plate and welded together. The M3A3 used a new power source in the form of the Twin General Motors 6-71 Diesel Engines in a bid to limit fuel combustion due to battle damage. The M3A4 utilised the original riveted hull but with the Chrysler Multibank engine which would also turn up in the later M4A4 Sherman and finally the M3A5 variant paired the riveted hull format with the Twin 6-71 diesel motors. Which ever way round the Lee/Grant tank was produced, it was fundamentally flawed and the crews did not like them. If given the choice they hoped for a better designed tank. Privately, they did not want to work in them, they did not want to drive them, and did not want to get involved in a skirmish on the battlefield against Axis armour inside one despite the fact they now had a main gun which could take on the opposition and which at least boosted morale after previous experience with the outdated 2 and 6-pounders of earlier British Tanks.

Some design work had commenced in 1940 experimenting with mounting the 75mm gun in a turret with 360 degree rotation. It would have to be mounted on a tank which used as many M3 tank parts as possible as this was already in production: road wheels, suspension, track, engines. The result of this work materialized on 16 September 1941 in the form of the Medium Tank T6. A cast hull and turret built around a short barrelled 75mm gun. The gun had two large muzzle weights fixed around the end of the barrel used to simulate the full mass of a larger gun when being tested, the 75mm M3 Gun which was used in final production models. There were two fixed Browning machine guns in the front hull, plus another which could be rotated in its ball mount also in the hull. Vertical volute suspension was used from the M3 Lee tank, with track return rollers mounted at the top centre of each bogie. These fittings can be noted on Michael in photograph IWM KID 1234. With further development the T6 became the standardized medium M4 Tank in October of 1941. By early 1942 it was in full production as the M4 and was being shipped to all campaign theatres. It was first tested in combat with the British Eighth Army in October that year during the battles of El Alamein, considered so secret a weapon at the time troops were instructed to refer to is by its codename THE SWALLOW. Later combat road testing took place in the TORCH landings by US forces in Algeria. The M4 vastly improved upon the M3 Medium tank design and consequently was used to replace the obsolete M3. Crew feedback was again consulted. With a much lower silhouette, a crew position eliminated and an assistant driver catered for plus the bigger gun and faster cross country ability the Sherman tank was adopted for the duration by all Allied armoured units. The following chapters reveal how the Sherman tank in its many variant forms contributed to Allied victory on all fronts. You will view some of the 49,000 or so Sherman tanks produced during the Second World War in the chapters included in this book.

Chapter Three

The UK Home Army – First UK Sherman to the 'Funny'

In the middle of 1940 the Home Army in Britain was bracing itself in preparation for a dispersed and defensive role fighting in the villages and streets of the South Coast in a potentially outnumbered and outgunned effort to repel German Invasion troops. As the German amphibious assault on the UK mainland faded following the Luftwaffe's defeat in the Battle of Britain, as Hitler's focus on Russia crystalized, collective pressures remained on the army structure at home. Britain's tanks during this period had proven totally inadequate – the A13 Cruisers, Matilda Mk I's and Mark VIB Light Cavalry Tanks were outgunned, out dated and mechanically obsolete. 7th Armoured Division of Wavell's Desert Army reported in September of 1940 that is was rare that even 200 of their 306 tanks could be operational at any one time due to breakdown from excessive desert mileage and lack of spares. A short respite had been granted with Hitler's focus elsewhere. It was only with the Matilda MkII with its 80mm armour, impervious to any Italian Gun in the desert that British armoured forces began to equip themselves with the right kit. Supremacy lasted until the *Afrika Korps* began employing their 88mm Flak Cannon in an anti-tank role. From 1941 onwards the Home Army in the UK faced two major objectives which were to equip and train the forces that would defeat the Axis Powers and bring the war to a victorious close. However, for British armoured forces training in the UK toward this end there seemed to be continuous and significant pressures imposed upon them. The *Lend-Lease Act* of 11 March, 1941 created the opportunity to re-equip on a large scale. By late 1942 the Sherman tank was proving itself at the hands of the men of the Eighth Army producing the 'turning tide' victory at El Alamein, however there was still huge argument about the application of the new tank. At home the first Shermans did not begin to appear through Lease Lend in any numbers until the summer of 1943 when all home-based armoured divisions were re-equipped with them. After the new tanks, came waiting for spare parts to keep them running, and further debate as to how best use the new tank on the battlefield. Not until mid 1943 did changes in armoured tactics filter down to training sessions, and these were directly attributable to analysis of desert campaign performance. Texts and training were concentrating on the use of armour alongside infantry whereas previously in the desert the armour had been seen as a self sufficient battlefield weapon. The War Office's publications of the time paid no attention to the arrival of this new tank in the education of troops nor did they explain the significant tactical improvements for the troops who had only trained on Churchills or Matildas.

Shortages of all items across the country due to industrial action, supply line stoppages, black market activity, rising costs coupled with cautious suspicion about wear and tear on irreplaceable and valuable vehicles plagued the preparation of Britain's armoured forces. Some units were unable to run their tanks for months at a time due to fear of mechanical damage, and stringent track wear regulations were subsequently set by the War Office. They enforced limits on mileage travelled to and from exercises. More importantly, heavy restrictions were placed on the amount of ammunition that could be drawn for exercise in an attempt to slow gun-barrel wear. Limited live round firing was permitted, few live rounds were issued to new crews and consequently their experience of accurate and rapid live firing suffered. Even the land to train armoured forces was virtually non-existent in 1941 and only by mid-war when Shermans were arriving in bulk, had they begun to become established. By this time however, holding camps and training areas were also in demand for the armies who had arrived in Britain to join the war effort. Huge formations of American, Canadian and Polish Divisions also required space for equipment, and to aid training.

Other problems with training can be viewed as simply unavoidable and were agreed and accepted at the time. Even at the most sophisticated battle school of the time, the real experience of armoured combat could never be replicated exactly. There was no substitute for genuine combat experience – one can note the increasing camouflage and addition of track sections, logs, road wheels, and cement to protect and disguise the hull utilised by Sherman crews as the campaigns progress in later chapters but how could this possibly have been prepared for on Salisbury Plain. Lessons though were being learnt and passed on from crew to crew.

In these early photographs however, the tanks arriving from the United States are still a novelty, seen here introduced to royalty and the press. Initial shots even show how unprepared the army was to collect the new tanks from the dockside! Private hauliers were contracted to collect the 40 ton leviathons in 1942 until later purpose built railroad cars were manufactured. Much of these early training photos show the men familiarizing themselves with the new tank, and this is exactly how it happened. With no real guidance in text other than technical repair alluded to in the maintenance manuals, and little change to command doctrine passed down by senior officers it was left to the divisions themselves to train their crews in tactics for the new tank by each individual unit preference.

Sherman tanks in British service looked much as they did in American service externally and other than viewing the internal fittings it can be quite a task pinpointing identifications. The exception to the rule was the Sherman Firefly types that Britain installed its 17-pounder high velocity cannon into. The elongated barrel and distinctive egg shaped muzzle brake often provide easy recognition of this type.

British Army nomenclature for the Sherman range also differed from the American terminology as the tables in the final chapter of this book demonstrate. The M4 to M4A4 variants were renamed by the British as the Sherman I to V. The late production Sherman Hybrid I in British terminology referred to the late production M4 which used a cast upper hull front and welded rear – hence 'Hybrid.' Weaponry was also categorized by letter suffixes A, B, and C which were used to represent 76mm gun, 105mm howitzer and the 17-pounder respectively. The letter Y was also applied in this system, denoting a late war model with HVSS (Horizontal Volute Spring Suspension). Therefore British designation for a Sherman M4A2 model with 76mm gun and HVSS would be classed as a SHERMAN IIIAY.

British Shermans can also often be identified in this book by considering the additional stowage applied in the UK. Often a large bin has been attached to the rear of the turret, and a long bin is attached to the hull plate. In photos just after the Normandy invasion this particular bin is often relocated to the front hull to create the space required by the wading funnel apparatus attached to the rear of the tanks which were waterproofed by D-Day. Other modifications were made individually or personally by crews. Track sections become increasingly apparent welded to the hulls of tanks as the campaign in Europe progressed. Some British tanks in Belgium clearly sport large sections of Churchill tank track section which must have been just about the heaviest item they could lay hands on to protect against anti-tank hollow charge rounds.

Radio aerials provide further clues to British service as American forces used entirely different radio equipment to our own. British tanks were fitted with the famous No.19 Set mounted inside the rear of the turret bustle. The 19 Set operated in two definitive modes requiring separate aerials which protruded from the turret. The A aerial was installed through the standard aerial socket and appears in photographs as a black rubber flexible cone, with aerial sections secured inside by wing-nut. The B aerial was secured through a small square socket to right of the bustle roof at the back of the turret. The twin set 19 radio equipment could provide short wave comms between tanks on the move with voice range of 1 to 5 miles, and the more powerful A set pushed voice communication further to a distance of 10 to 15 miles. British tank commanders in North Africa were also fond of flying pennants from both aerials and not just for decoration. Inter-war training had hammered home the necessity of sending semiphore , signalling by flag, and indeed the pennant sent message was a leftover from the Infantry Tanks of the Great War. Lessons were soon learnt however that a tank flying colourful pennants must be of command significance and would become a primary enemy target.

The turrets of British tanks also sometimes had a single 2 inch smoke bomb thrower fitted, or brackets welded to the side of the turret to fit twin 4 inch dischargers. Many were fitted with a thoughtful if easily damaged rear view driver's mirror – an example of this has been photographed in the Normandy chapter. Two Methyl Bromide fire extinguishers were added to either side of the rear decking, and a small first aid kit also in a tin was welded onto the rear hull plate. Finally I refer again to those personal touches – a unique addition to the turret of the Shermans in service with the Coldstream Guards in Holland (captured in photos featured in this book) are the fitting of Typhoon Rockets and their firing rails, directly taken off the aircraft, and applied to the tank beefing up its weaponry considerably. Practical consideration however does beg the question of effectiveness and of indeed aiming the rockets.

This is how the Sherman tank and a few of its predecessors looked in British Service on duty with the Home Army while the training for later campaigns in NW Europe was about to begin.

Early Lease-Lend arrivals in June of 1942 are paraded for the press. Front view of new M3 Lee tank, exhibiting riveted hull construction and British Army modifications on this model. Stowage box under main gun, and early mud chutes are fitted between road wheel supporting bogies to deflect the build up of mud falling off the tracks. The bracket for British smoke dischargers has been fitted to the side of the turret and armoured plugs have been welded to the apertures of the obsolete fixed twin .30 bow machine gun ports. High cupola on turret distinguishes this Lee from the Grant Tank in British service. Specially designed rail cars have already been placed in use to transport armour around the country, but limitations of elevation and traverse of the main 75mm gun are instantly apparent when mounted in the sponson on the side of the tank. IWM H 20919

The same Lee tank rolls off a railcar for the press demonstration. Note additional auxiliary fuel drum tank mounted to the rear right of hull and rear view pistol port providing an aiming aperture for small arms fire over the rear deck. Smoke discharger bracket is again seen on left of turret, and the British have added another padlocked stowage box to the rear of the turret. Sherman heritage is exhibited by exhaust pipe layout and the access doors to the engine compartment, also bogies, road wheels and tracks. American and British troops explain the details to reporters. IWM H 20920

28 June, 1942. Lend lease Grant I's craned ashore with all apertures sealed for the Atlantic crossing. These were probably from the first batches of Grant tanks produced in the US by Pullman Standard or The Pressed Steel Car Company under direct British Contract. The high commander's turret cupola of the M3 Lee tank has been redesigned into a lower silhouette split hatch for the commander of the Grant turret by British Tank Mission request. Both will be towed away to be adapted and made serviceable before issue to British armoured forces at a Central Tank Park. Neither are fitted with headlights, tools, radios or have aerial mountings yet. Nor are the additional stowage boxes added under the main gun, or on the lid of the rear stowage box on the left of the engine deck. They exhibit the factory fitted sand shields however which were adopted on some Sherman models. British T census numbers have been sprayed on the hull at the factory as these AFV's were manufactured under British Government contract. IWM H21033

Civilian contractors tow away the newly arrived Grant I's on commercial trailers. Tyres manufactured from solid rubber had to be used in order to shoulder the weight of the tanks. New tanks meant redesigning new logistical support networks to transport and service them. The detail of the waterproofing compounds applied to all apertures is clearly visible, ensuring safe transit across the Atlantic where much of the armour was lashed down on open deck as well as stored within the holds of ships. The effects of the ocean's corrosive salty atmosphere was kept at bay by these measures. IWM H21062

Although not a focus for this book, here is a late production Canadian Ram II Tank fitted with 6-pdr being towed behind a Ram II ARV (Armoured Recovery Vehicle.) Again a press demonstration for American, Canadian and British journalists they film the ARV hooking onto the Ram Tank using a draw bar. Traditional wooden leverage spikes are also fitted to the side of the ARV. Sherman heritage is also clearly visible in bogie design, spoked road wheels, hull shape and other vision slot features. Although not used in action in a turret tank role, some of these Rams were adapted as Personnel Carriers and used in the recovery format. Photograph taken in the UK, March 1943. Of note on the ARV is the door hatch on the side of the hull, later deleted on Ram II hulls. IWM H 29336

The rear view of the Canadian Ram II ARV (Armoured Recovery Vehicle) revealing winches, jumbo storage boxes and the Hollibone designed draw bars. Interestingly rope is being utilised as well as steel hauser cable in these early recovery demonstrations. This view clearly demonstrates the Sherman's design references again though the RAM tanks used a wider track. Note the anchor attachments on track sections to grip when the tank was winching disabled vehicles in muddy conditions. IWM H29350

Lease Armour Begins Arriving in the UK...

Crated Sherman tank arrives in Liverpool Docks during December, 1942 under the Lease-Lend scheme. Crated up in the hold of a giant Liberty Ship, several methods of packaging the completed tanks were utilised including open storage on deck. The crates contained tracks and all external fittings for the tank and were nailed together in sections around the tank once it had been driven onto the base. Finally the edges of each section were sealed with black pitch visible in the photo, to guard against the weather. IWM H26261

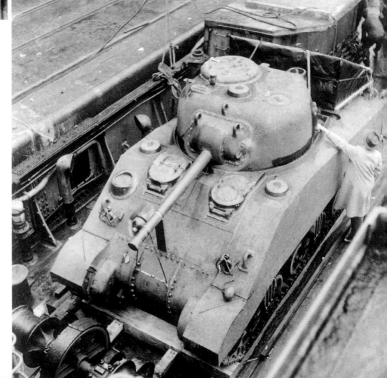

Other packaging methods are shown as more tanks arrive in Liverpool during 1942. For those tanks which would be stored in the open on deck, all apertures were sealed with a gripon or asbestos paste against Atlantic weather viewed around hatches, commander's turret ring and air vents. Headlights have remained fitted as is the siren for travelling. This is an early Sherman M4 model and is prepared for craning onto the harbour-side as the foreman stevedore checks the security of the spares crate on the rear deck of the tank.. A good view of the early M34 gun mount and shield, with pronounced lifting rings, three part front transmission cover and the 'comb' attachment under the hull machine gun mount is of note. This comb feature is examined in depth in the next photograph. IWM H 26255

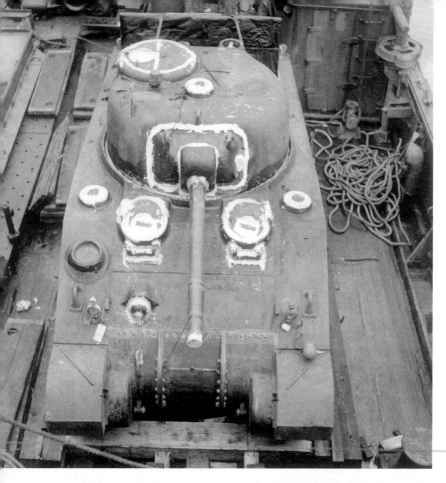

White asbestos paste seals all apertures on this Sherman M4 which arrived in Liverpool. Of special note here is the evidence which now informs on the use of the 'comb' feature, a small bracket welded on the front left section of the transmission cover. The 'comb' has long been a source of mystery to the Sherman enthusiast, and its purpose lost to history. Here we can clearly see that the bracket, which had four of five groves cut into it, was used as an adjustable anchor point to a securing cable and plug which fitted into the hull mg mount position. This stopped the ball mount rolling with the pitch of the waves at sea , or when being craned on and off ship, thus avoiding breaking the asbestos sealant, and allowing sea air or water into the hull during its journey across the Atlantic. Headlights remain fitted without blackout covers, and siren is wired onto the driver's side front wing. IWM H 26256

Once ashore, and checked over in the Central Tank Parks, the Shermans were issued to the troops who set to work devising new working practices in keeping the tank operational in the field. An early M4 Sherman is used in recovery training as a Grant ARV reverses back to connect with a Hollibone drawbar in use. Note early T48 rubber block tracks with rubber chevron cuff, 75mm barrel packed full of grease, and no hull mg fitted. Front vision slots can be seen at the front of the driver's and co driver's hatches as well as periscope mounting on the inside of the hatch lids. These vision slots were later deleted in favour of periscope view only. A Challenger/Cromwell hybrid ARV charges by sporting a mini turret similar to Canal Defence adapted models. IWM H 27580

The young trooper in control of the recovery exercise guides the driver of the Grant ARV back to engage the drawbar, speaking to the driver via external connection to the ARV crew intercom. Shermans seen in the Far East chapter utilise the later Interphone Box, BC-1362 with Cordage CO213 on the rear hull plate of each tank so that infantry shielding behind could talk direct to the crew inside the tank via telephone handset and direct fire support themselves. Note the white paint on the Grant's track. This indicated quick recognition for tank and repair crews of the position the tank should be for easier manual removal of the tracks.
IWM H 27577

The draw bar is secured through the Sherman's towing eyes, welded to the front transmission plate. Many later Shermans are seen fitted in the field with a number of large U shackles to facilitate a range of easy towing options. Hauser towing cables were also adopted and stored connected on the hull ready for a quick tow if required. T48 Rubber track blocks are already showing some wear and a good view of the two part Sherman headlight should be noted. The standard US Army sidelight was mounted above the headlight with blackout slot cover, through the casing. Both units were removable when the tank was going into a frontline situation, and were released by pulling a fixing pin from inside the hull. They would then either be stored in the holder attached to the headlight guard, secured by the chain seen hanging next to the light, or were brought inside the tank.
IWM H27578

'Michael' the second production M4A1 tank manufactured at the Lima Locomotive Works in Ohio and the first Sherman M4A1 to arrive in the UK for active service. The name of the tank was derived from Sir Michael Dewar's christian name after he lead the British Tank Mission to the US in order to secure Grant contracts from American manufacturers on behalf of the British Government. Of note are the early or first type bogies with return rollers fitted in the top centre, spoked road wheels, the removal of the twin fixed bow machine guns and the fitting of new M3 75mm main gun. The pistol port in the turret is clearly visible and Michael is fitted with early T51 tracks using large rectangular flat rubber track blocks. 'Michael' survived the war and sixty years on is now exhibited at The Tank Museum, Bovington, UK in superb condition. IWM KID 1234

The Queen and daughter Princess Elizabeth view a Sherman of 11th Armoured Division. Note the camouflage scheme applied to front hull. This photograph provides a good view of casting numbers on the transmission cover. These provided part number and manufacturer information, often giving clues to Foundry locations. It had either recently rained, or a gloss finish has been applied for the Royal inspection. Alongside the bull motif of 11th Armoured Division is a painted circle indicating this tank belonged to C Squadron. Symbols to denote armoured squadron identification included a white diamond to indicate HQ Squadron, a red triangle to A Squadron, a yellow square notifying B Squadron and solid white block for D Squadron. Colour coding was not rigid and individual units adapted these basic instructions in a variety of ways, applying them in locations from turret to front wing. Additional track types become more apparent in photographs as the war progresses. Tracks fitted to this Sherman are of the T54 E2 type, which were of all steel construction, utilising a curved edge cuff. IWM H 36974

M4A2 Shermans on exercise delivered by flat rail cars on the LNER Line from Newmarket to Cambridge. The crews would be transported in passenger carriages attached to the last of the flat cars. All exhibit squadron markings of C squadron, and now have blackout covers fitted over main headlights although divisional signs are obscured by dust. The lead tank has the British developed cast steel T51 Track fitted which differs to the others that are fitted with sandshields. It is possible this tank was fitted specially with these tracks to compare durability with the other tanks in the squadron. The welded manufacture of the M4A2 driver's hood seen in this photograph on the front tank can be contrasted with cast types on other models. Steel hauser towing cables are now secured on every hull. IWM H 37573

In March, 1943 a large tank demonstration was conducted at Lulworth Camp for a VIP audience. An early British M4A2 Sherman accepted for service sports red and white tricolour 'Armoured Force' identification, and T Census numbers painted along the hull and across the single rounded nose transmission cover. Steel towing cable and U shackles are now also fitted to the towing eyes in the transmission cover. Early vision slots are still visible, along with the blade or vane sight mounted on the front of the turret top in front of the commander's hatch. This could provide an immediate orientation guide for the commander as he emerged from the turret to observe direction. IWM H 28344

By April 1944, Tank Storage Parks were working at full capacity in preparation for invasion. This one, No. 8 AFV Depot, located in Leicester repairs M4 and M4A2 models. Appliqué armour is welded on to the hulls while the barrel is cleaned by another fitter. Headlights have been removed as has bow machine gun. IWM H 37820

British army assembly and repair depot, days before the invasion in Normandy. Nearest the camera is an M4A4 variant, with British added stowage box on the rear of the turret. M4A6's are present in background with extended exhaust covers as is a lone Cromwell tank and a line of Bren Gun carriers. Workshop van races up and down the lines of Armour dropping off spare parts and mechanics who hurry to ready the vehicles for D-Day. Note the five pointed Allied Invasion Star marking has not yet been applied to a single vehicle. IWM H 38922

D-Day preparations on the south coast in late May, 1944. All of these tanks marked up with large 18" high red numbers with 1" white outlines on the turrets belong to C Squadron, 13/18 Hussars. The Sea Horse of 27th Armoured Brigade is visible on the one piece transmission cover of nearest tank, as is the chalked on numbering system indicating it would be loaded onto LST 3. 'Charmer', tank 68 also visible has two panels of appliqué armour added to its hull, and both sport bomb throwers mounted in front of the commanders ring on the top of the turret. They also wear weatherproof canvas covers for the main gun and mounting. Canvas muzzle covers are also fitted. Additional sections of track have been fitted to both sides of each turret. Steel T54E2 tracks are fitted and the Sherman nearest camera has a mixture of spoked and solid wheels fitted, spares are strapped to the front hull too. IWM H 38970

To The South – 27th Armoured Brigade tanks, all fitted with T51 British steel track, move from Petworth to Gosport for loading. All road signs indicate one route only, here a column of Shermans already chalked up with loading instructions on the transmission covers heads for the embarkation ports. Draw bar is mounted across the front of the hull, periscopes are fitted in the front hatch doors, spare wheels and return roller, and bundled kit are all tied down. The lead tank looks to rendezvous with LCT Number 4. Appliqué armour patches are clearly visible along side the hull of each tank. (1 June 1944.) IWM H 38985

Reversing an A Squadron, 1st E. Riding Yeomanry Sherman from 27th Armoured Brigade fitted with wading trunk into an LST pre D-Day. No.1 is fully laden for assault with spare wheels, solid disc and hollow spoke, draw bars, blocks of wood and a .30 MG tripod all fastened on to the front hull. (1 June 1944.) Exhaust fumes blast out from the trunk fitted to the rear of the tank. Weight, Height , Width and Length shipping data is stencilled near the driver's position and Loading instructions listing which LST this vehicle would be loaded onto has been chalked on under the co-driver. The crew wear goggles over their berets, battledress tunic and trousers and sidearms on webbing belts. IWM H 38978

Milk for the embarking troops of M4A2 'Challenger', of 13/18 Hussars. Note weatherproof mantle cover for the sea crossing, bracket for smoke dischargers on side of turret, and the good view provided of the T51 Steel track. The wading funnel for the exhaust system is just visible, and interestingly this Sherman is fitted with the very early centrally mounted return roller on each bogie. IWM H 38988

Development and Use of 'Funnies' in the Home Army

'Rita' — an experimental M4 Fascine Carrier, intended to catapult the trench filler constructed of long timbers bolted together into any trench or hole in the path of advancing armoured forces. The carrier assembly could be unbolted later and the tank returned to normal combat role, or in an emergency the turret could be rotated and the fitted structure knocked out of the way. IWM H 31830 & IWM H 31829

(4 April 1945) This example of the Sherman TWABY Assault Bridge was photographed in Italy, however this 'funny' was developed in the UK as a temporary bridging solution. Essentially a turret-less Chassis with folding ramps running the length of the hull. King posts held up the ramps and deployed them at measured speed via pulley. When fully outstretched the TWABY could form a bridge across a river, ditch or anti-tank obstacle allowing vehicles from jeep to tank weights to cross. Note the long track extenders fitted to provide more traction in muddy terrain. Photographs exist of these in use throughout the Italian campaign. IWM NA 23763

A 79th Armoured Division Special – 'Chief', a Sherman M4 Fascine Carrier sporting rubber mould T48 tracks. The fascine was a proven method of overcoming ditch and uneven shell damaged terrain dating back to the First War. Clearly this frontal view demonstrates how the bundled fence stakes would roll down the framework welded to the front of the hull and position the fascine directly in front of the chassis. Note the flex aerial mounting on the left of the front hull glacis plate allowing flexing as the fascine roll travelled by. The quick release mechanism is also seen. IWM NA 23770

Beach Armoured Recovery Vehicles – 'BARV Shermans'

Both types of Beach Armoured Recovery Vehicles (BARV) designed by the British are shown in these photographs. H35624 shows the most recognisable BARV with high additional armoured superstructure. Several of this type used on D-Day have survived into preservation by private owners or are exhibited in museums including the D-Day Museum, Southsea, UK.
IWM H 35624

IWM H 33078 demonstrates the much rarer BARV which featured a square dummy turret, and tall wading box vent on the rear of the hull being used on invasion exercises in the spring of 1944. The stencilling alongside the T census number reads 'This vehicle is filled with antifreeze and must not be drained.' A jeep fitted with large speaker travels along the beach behind the tank issuing instruction for the troops already landed.

The AMRCR demonstrating full ploughing depth as the castor rollers are lost in the soil. AMRCR stood for 'Anti-Mine Reconnaissance Castor Rollers' version. The rollers provided plenty of depth and disturbance to detonate many variants of explosive from anti-personnel to anti-tank mine. Main gun and bow MG are also unobstructed for normal usage. IWM H 34219

Despite the paper label attached to the turret reading 'CRAB' this is in fact a Sherman AMRCR on test, originally an M4A4 variant.. Tests proved that as the castors made furrows through a minefield they detonated the munitions and in absorbing the blast would individually detach themselves from the frame work. In its path lay a clear passageway through any danger. This meant that the tank could continue sweeping clear paths through a minefield before being refitted with more castor rollers. H33677 gives a good detailed view of the simple rivet and girder construction of the lifting arms, and a view of another M4A4 variant distinguishing feature. Let your eyeline follow the turret splash guard between the hull and turret from left to right, and you will notice a small square plate welded onto the splash guard. This was added on M4A4 variants to protect the drainage holes along the guard and only appears on the M4A4 model.
IWM H 33674 & IWM H 33677

Shermans also assisted in the design process of other funnies. Here a Churchill ARK with additional trackway added to its hull assists a Sherman M4A4 to piggy back over a sea wall obstacle and into the battle during a training exercise in preparation for Normandy.
IWM H 36601

Flail drum damage demonstrated. After continued use flailing fields all day in army demonstrations. The hull and turret are coated in mud from the mine clearing activity. Barbed wire cutting discs can be seen at either end of drum. IWM H 34408

Crab type flail Sherman at a demonstration day. Note the mud splattering in H34200. The flail device is interesting as it is not of the design regularly seen on Crab II Shermans, and is more close in design to those seen on Sherman Marquis experimental types and on some Crab I's. It is most likely an experimental version of the Crab I flail tank with wire cutting devices located at either end of the roller. Too weak to carry the roller weight self-sufficiently, the experimental roller is 'piggy-backed' on the rear deck of a second Sherman. 43 flailing chains were fitted and each chain weighed between 21 and 23lbs. The total weight of rotor drum was circa 13cwt. Stronger hydraulic arms were required!
IWM H34198 & IWM H 34200

Less well recognised than the Jeffries Plough mine clearance attachment is this version of the Bull's Horns Plough, being tested by 79th Armoured Division prior to D-Day. The 79th Divisional Sign can be seen on the front transmission cover along with bridge classification of 40 stencilled in white, and repainted in black on a small yellow circle to the left. The plough was inspired by British agricultural equipment that graded the soil as opposed to creating furrows but was deemed ineffective for actual combat issue and was dropped in the testing phase. The Jeffries Plough differred in that the mine locating plates were flat. IWM H 36602

Churchill inspects a Guards Armoured Tank unit before D-Day in an M3 half-track resplendent in gloss camouflage scheme, and fitted with review stand framework in the rear body. Note the Houseboat fittings on the front of each tank which facilitated the erection of a camouflage screen above the tank disguising it from air observation to appear as a straightforward three-ton lorry – the Sherman was now an accepted and well respected element of British Armoured Forces. These are M4A4 variants.
IWM H 37165

Chapter Four

North Africa – British Action Egypt, Libya, Tunisia

The loss of equipment at Dunkirk in 1940 followed by defeat at Gazala, followed by further loss of men and equipment at Tobruk was the catalyst for the introduction of the Sherman tank into the British Army. Prime Minister Winston Churchill received confirmation of the defeat at Tobruk in the presence of President Roosevelt while in Washington. As Roosevelt offered assistance Churchill had only the one request – send as many of the new Sherman tanks as could be spared immediately to North Africa. General Marshall was summoned to the White House and the possibility was fervently explored. Marshall's initial response was to ship a complete American armoured division straight out to Egypt and the then Major General George S Patton Jr. was ordered to return from the Desert Training Center and mobilize the 2nd Armoured Division for shipment as of immediate effect. The Sherman tank had only recently been standardized and was only then coming into full factory production, so the 2nd Armoured were forced to mix and match tanks from other units to mass at full strength. However, when shipping schedules were investigated further issues arose as it was discovered it would be mid November before the division might arrive in Egypt and this could only be achieved if they survived the crossing while hunted by the U-Boat fleet. The desperate turn of events in North Africa deemed the date of arrival too late to be thought effective in stopping Rommel's advance.

An alternative plan consisted of sending some three hundred Shermans taken off troops training with them in the continental USA and to ship them sooner, with an additional 100 self-propelled 105mm Howitzers and this was carried out on 15 July 1942 in a special freight convoy from the US. Only a day later one of the ships was torpedoed and sunk and so fifty-two additional tanks were also sent to replenish the loss. Nearly two months later the first 318 tanks intended for combat with the British Army were put ashore at Tel el Kebir in Egypt consisting mainly of M4A1 type with M4A2 in much smaller numbers. The troops awaiting the new armour had already had an opportunity to familiarize themselves with the new weapon as a single Sherman M4A1, armed with the shorter barrelled 75mm M2 gun had arrived some weeks before in enforced secrecy.

British workshops set to work preparing the new shipment of tanks using their experience of desert warfare to date. To their own design, tailored sand shields were added to most of the tanks which were later adopted at the factory at time of manufacture albeit to a slightly altered shape. Constructed of thin sheet steel the intention was to deflect the clouds of dust created by the vehicle in motion. This work however was incomplete by October of 1942 when Montgomery was eager to launch the battle at El Alamein. The Eighth Army had 252 operational Shermans on the start line for the battle, and the remainder of the original 318 shipped out were spread around in the rear units or remained unserviceable in the workshops awaiting parts. These tanks had to be disguised from aerial or mountain top observation as they formed up and a top secret plan named 'Sun Shield' was put into operation. This involved a welded and bolted framework being fitted around the girth of the tank that would support a larger square tent like framework and canvas on which the physical attributes of a three ton lorry could be painted. The plan was a resounding success and many of the photographs in this and Chapter 5 demonstrate that the basic frame supports still existed on many of the tanks in case this ruse was required again at a later stage in the war. Of course tanks of other manufacture (780) made up the majority of the armour force for the battle. Some units only received tanks the day before the offensive such were the tight deadlines being worked to.

The first ever tank to tank engagement of the Sherman took place against elements of 15th Panzer Division shortly after the start. Approaching directly toward advancing Shermans of 2nd Armoured Division, who were picking their way through the foot soldiers of the 51st Highland Division the action got underway. German tanks were identified as Panzer III's and IV's and engaged at a range of 2,000 yards. A brief exchange of fire took place creating damage on both sides before the enemy retreated in the opposite direction to the advance: Lost to the wider historical record of the war, but not to those that were there, or to those who were gauging the performance of the new tank on both sides of the Atlantic. The tank's undisputed success in further action throughout the course of the Alamein battle and in North Africa assured that the Sherman would receive adoption by British forces everywhere the war would be fought, and would be sent everywhere American Armoured Forces would be in action.

As the last Axis prisoner fell into allied hands during May of 1943 the three year campaign in the desert drew to a close. The arrival and capture of Cap Bon on the Tunisian coast on 13 May had cemented the notion of the turning tide first embraced by the British public after the victory at Alamein in October 1942. The photographs in this chapter help capture the first Sherman tanks in British and Commonwealth service during that vital period of the war. Technical features such as British designed stowage bins, and sand shields, the camouflage schemes and unit markings, the desert landscapes and fighting conditions are all recorded. Visits from inquisitive VIP's, instruction from American Sherman Experts, British training on the new tank, battle damaged tanks and the culminating Victory parades in Cairo and Tunis all convey the story of the tank's initiation into the British Army.

West of Agheila, Christmas celebrations were conducted in the Tripolitanian Desert during December, 1942. With holly and berries chalk-drawn onto their M4 turret and bunting made of torn newspaper this tank crew enjoy a Christmas meal as two German prisoners are marched away to captivity enviously glancing over at the food from home! IWM E 20571

December, 1942. 'When in doubt – brew up!' A crew gather to read the tea leaves and share a cigarette in between spells of duty within reach of their M4A1 variant, which exhibits centrally mounted first type return rollers on the top of each bogie. Examples of additional British storage bins are also seen. IWM E 21330

Benghazi in January, 1943. American mechanics assigned from US Armoured Forces help rectify early teething troubles with some of the first Shermans in British Service. British MP Jack Lawson (MP for Chester-Le-Street, Co. Durham) watches the men at work at a REME repair depot in the back streets. The party went on a tour of Tobruk, taking in the memorials to the siege and inspecting the harbour. The censor has obliterated all identification markings other than the full size '43' painted on the turret side. M4A1's are parked in the front row and an M4 is being worked on. IWM E 21472

American Tank Experts in Tripolitania observe how their product (Sherman M4A1, Sherman II's) perform in action with the British Army, explain the finer points of the working Sherman. These were part of the first shipments to reach North Africa. Black camouflage scheme has been quickly applied with a spray gun as they examine the tank for battle damage. Among the US party was Lieutenant General Jacob L. Devers, America's number one tank expert in the Middle East. (Undated) IWM E 20690

West of Marble Arch British armour and infantry set off to chase the retreating DAK after fierce clashes. Infantry now partnered with the new M4 Sherman tank and are ferried into battle. The troops have to take cover on the rear deck, burnt by sun and hot engine, they find a position providing low silhouette amidst track hammers, shovels, pick axes and a track spike – part of the Sherman's on board track maintenance kit strapped to the rear decking. Note detail of British applied rear turret stowage box. IWM E 20505

'Cocky' – an M4A2, Sherman III destroyed by enemy action outside Benghazi. The sand shield on the right side of tank has been blown out at a right angle to hull and two impact points can be noted above the centre bogie. All the stowage bins have been opened and searched. Note the 'opening halves' nature of the stowage box mounted on the rear of the turret. The number 06 has been painted over with a black circle with an oblique line – signifying 'knocked out' to any passing vehicles. The intensity of the fire has bent the aerials but the remnants of the tank's pennant still flies. Blackened sand is visible around the wreck due to intense fire within the vehicle. IWM E 20574

RAC School at Abbassia. Photographed by Sgt. Chetwyn on 19 January, 1943 this shot shows a special course in progress given to tank men in the handling and maintenance of all types of tank. This is the Sherman Engine maintenance class, checking the oil filters and air cleaners, tapping them out to clean them against the side of the hull. (Note staining!) IWM E21382

The finer details of the commander's turret ring are explained inside a Sherman at the RAC School at Abbassia. (19 January, 1943.) Note the leather padding, sponge and horsehair filled and samples of white interior paint finish on hatch door and inner hull to maximise reflection of light inside the tank. IWM E 21386

Final instruction at Abbassia culminated in a 'rough-riding' course for all tank men. The Shermans were sent over some of the rougher, undulating desert terrain at speed. Late production version of M4A2. Bow machine guns have been eliminated, cast one piece transmission cover, and second type bogies with return rollers on trailing side can be seen. Note blade sight and other sighting devices on turret top. The 'closing halves' type stowage box is attached to the rear of the turret. (19th January, 1943.) IWM E 21393

The final advance of the Eighth Army in Libya. Three columns pushed forward, one along the main road two inland to stop Rommel making anything more than a brief stand during his fighting retreat. Moving toward Tripoli, Dominion, and Home County regiments fought alongside each other. Here Trooper Fred Lee of Reading, of The Sherwood Rangers is captured through the lens. A veteran of the desert campaign in Egypt and now Libya he halts his tank for the cameraman. Eyes protected by his goggles this desert tank driver is caked in sand and dust . Trooper Lee was a peacetime lorry driver before the war.
IWM E21499

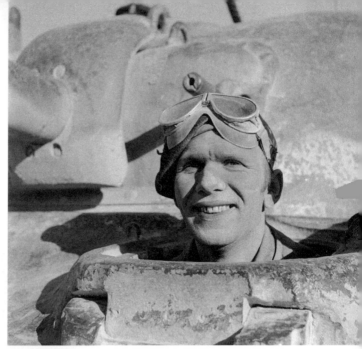

The commander faired a little better from the dust coating that his driver received but creates an exposed silhouette on top of the turret as demonstrated in this shot. Described as a typical Tank Man by the original caption this is Lieutenant Ted Phelan of Streatham, London. He has also advanced all the way from Alamein and will soon be on the streets of Tripoli! Details of the early M34 gun mount for the 75mm main gun are clearly visible.
IWM E 21500

Sherman M4A1 (II) tanks race across a desert floor of rocks, grit and sand in open ground toward Tripoli. Often brief rainfall overnight would turn a landscape such as this into an instant carpet of flowers. Seeds carried on the desert winds could instantly bloom and within a few hours of arid daytime heat wilt and die off again creating an alien environment for the British tankers to come to terms with.
IWM E 21503

5 April 1943 in Aleppo. Lieutenant General W G Holmes, CB, DSO, G.O.C 9th Army paying a visit to 10th Armoured Division on an informal visit. There was a short parade of vehicles through Aleppo but no formal parade. Here a Sherman M4A1 fires down a range as senior officers look on. .303 Bren Light Machine Gun is used as a ranging aid and conserves heavier 75mm ammunition. IWM E 23457

General Alexander and Lieutenant General McCreery (who ended the war as G.O.C 8th Army in 1945) host a tour from the Turkish Military Mission led by Turk General Omurtag of armoured units in the Tebesa area at 18th Army Group Headquarters. The Turkish Mission were permitted to inspect a Sherman M4A2 and were given a battle display by 6th Armoured Division men. IWM E 23723

Excellent parade demonstration of this late Tripolitanian campaign camouflage scheme exhibited by 6th Armoured Division as the Turkish Mission departs after the display. M4A2 Crews on the left throw salutes as the staff cars pass. IWM E 23724

Victory parade in Cairo on 14 June 1943 covered by AFPU men Captain Cash, Lieutenant McLaren, Sgt Lotzof and Sgt Oldham. Five thousand troops, with tanks, armoured cars and soft-skin vehicles drove through the city. Squadrons of RAF fighter planes swooped low in salute to the flags of the thirty-four United Nations of the period. General Sir Henry Maitland Wilson, C-in-C, MEF took the salute during which he presented Victoria Cross ribbons to two officers Brigadier LM Campbell and Major H W Le Patourel. The M4A2, with single cast transmission cover, was at the very head of columns, and led the parade in honour of its service in the Western Desert. IWM E 25247

15 October, 1943. The Rt. Hon. Robert Anthony Eden, MC, MP, Secretary of State for Foreign Affairs spends a few days in Cairo on his way to Moscow for a 'Big Three' Conference. He took time out to specifically visit British tank regiments and is seen here with men and tanks of the Yorks Hussars. IWM E 26151

Eden is informed about the technical specifications of the new tank and was fascinated by radio communication between vehicles. He was given the opportunity to listen in to a conversation between two tank commanders of the 4th Yorks Hussars, as a mix of M4's and M4A2's are parked up in the rear IWM E 26157

Eden sits on the 'half and half' stowage box fixed to the rear of this Sherman turret, amidst the short and long range aerials and was soon inside the tank having the crew stations explained in detail. The original caption of the period suggests 'the popular Foreign Secretary obviously enjoyed chatting to the tank men' and this is clear to see. IWM E 26156

Victory parades take place at the close of the Tripolitanian campaigns. M4 Tanks of the 3rd Hussars, and 1st RHA who constituted 9th Armoured Brigade amongst others parade past Brigadier Cameron and Lieutenant General Anderson with Major General Norman on the saluting base. British Armoured Brigade strength is demonstrated in these photographs. IWM E 26199

Camo scheme details are revealed as the display forms up, and additional views of the sun shield framework, sirens and headlights plus barrel camouflage which appears to be an early forerunner of the later W/O counter shading schemes applied to 17-pounder barrels.
IWM E 26201

Another view of the same parade forming provides views of British adapted wing stowage baskets on M4A2's, the use of pennants on aerials and the naming of tanks. 'Defiant' sits centre stage, with triangle squadron marking blending into camouflage scheme. IWM E 26200

M4A2 in urban combat after months in the desert. Forward elements of the First Army enter Tunis and take fire from an enemy strongpoint in this half built block of flats. Heavy armour was brought up to deal with the situation, with the help of infantry support. After a sharp and brief engagement the enemy were subdued. Note the darker paint scheme late in the campaign.(7 May 1943)
IWM NA 2536

'Adamant' leads as Shermans rumble by in a cloud of dust in front of another victory parade saluting base. Note identically patterned camouflage schemes on each tank.
IWM E 26207

Alternate view of desert drive past featuring both M4A2's and M4's.
IWM E 26208

Final victory parade in Tunis on 20 May 1943. Units from all the Allied Forces had participated in this parade and the salute was taken by General Eisenhower, General Alexander, General Anderson and General Giraud. Pipers of the 51st Highland Division led these M4 and M4A2 Sherman tanks of the Scots Guards past the saluting base. Conflict in North Africa was over! IWM NA 3016A

Chapter Five

The Mediterranean – Sicily and the Hop to Italy

Many of the Sicilian and Italian invasion shots show the tanks waterproofed for amphibious landing. A veteran of 7th Armoured Division told me that they were only shown how to prepare their tanks for landing a few weeks before the attack in Tripoli. This involved a group of men from the REME arriving one morning to demonstrate how the tank could be reversed into turret-deep water and driven out again with its engine still running. This amazing feat was achieved by fitting a cowling over the air intake, extending the exhausts to stick up skyward, and plugging all apertures with an asbestos paste including the driver's and machine gunner's hatch doors. The tank crews of 7th Armoured gathered on the waterline to laugh and cheer at the perceived disastrous demonstration, but sure enough, the tanks that had been water-proofed rolled down into the sea, and virtually submerged were able to halt with engine running. After shifting gear they slowly emerged until driven ashore again. 7th Armoured Division was not to go into action for the invasion of Sicily, but were represented by General Bobby Erskine and his TAC HQ on the day. However, lessons learnt provided valuable information for amphibious tank landings on other D-Days in Europe and the South Pacific.

10 July 1943 marked the date for the landings on the Sicilian coast. British Eighth Army troops who had crewed their Shermans through the North African battlefields would be ordered to press on with the offensive departing from Cap Bon and other ports with wading equipment attached to their tanks. They were expected to take the Island and then make the hop to the toe of the Italian mainland and pursue the Axis forces until Italy was free. Three days later the allied army was embedded on the island and some 50,000 Italian troops had been cut off by Patton with his capturing of Palermo and isolation of the northern end of the island. Ports and airfields were falling, and the liberation appeared to be occurring rapidly. Messina fell on 17 August and so did resistance on the island. By 19 August it was being reported that the Italian Sixth Army had lost 300,000 in the defence of the island but that the Italian mainland now only lay three miles away. The most important British adaptation to the Sherman tank is first seen in combatphotography originating after the coastal landings on the Italian mainland. The Firefly used by the British, and later New Zealand, Polish and Canadian forces housed the 17-pounder

high velocity cannon in a modified Sherman turret, and the addition of this gun created Allied armour in 1943 that could at last face up to anything the Germans could muster on the battlefield and destroy it. So, how did this innovative development come around? First mooted as early as 1941, the 17-pounder design had its origin in anti-tank gun development. Feedback from battles in North Africa and the realisation that Germany was introducing ever more heavily armoured tanks called for a weapon to fight back with. The first test model appeared in August 1942, and the first towed anti-tank guns were issued in Tunisia during January of 1943. Most of these arrived on 25-pounder carriages as their own purpose-built carriages were having production problems at the factories.

The Tank Division of the Ministry of Supply at first rejected calls to mount the gun in the amply available Shermans arriving by Liberty Ship in the UK by mid-1943. However, with the battlefield pressures of increasingly powerful German tanks they were forced to re-think, and ordered some initial experimentation. After further tests the scheme went ahead. The size of the gun created the biggest problem, or rather its housing in the standard turret of the tank designed with inches to spare for the smaller 75mm gun. A new mount and recoil system was required, but the old trunnions were utilised from the 75mm in true wartime spirit of making do. The radio set was moved into an armoured box welded to the exterior of the turret. Part of the turret was cut away inside to provide access in order to stop the larger 17-pounder breech recoiling back into it when fired. A distinctive egg shaped double baffle muzzle brake was threaded onto the end of the barrel and was often camouflaged in distinctive War Office counter-shaded paint scheme as is illustrated in both this and Chapter 6.

Other modifications had to be made to the tank to allow it to operate. The crew were reduced to four from five by removing the role of assistant driver. His crew station was remodellled to store additional ammunition, and of course without a crew member sat behind it the bow machine gun became obsolete. This was removed and the aperture for the mount was sealed with an armoured plug. This feature acts as a very good method of identifying those tanks in the Firefly mould. Test results from conduct in Italy ensured they would be present for the Normandy Invasion and the order went out to the Royal Ordnance factory to begin conversions. As many as twelve were issued to each British armoured regiment for the invasion. The Firefly remained present throughout the NW European campaign and are seen in the victory parades through Holland to Berlin.

After the loss of Sicily Mussolini was dismissed from office by Victor Emmanuel III and placed under arrest with an imposition of martial law. The Allies seized on this opportunity to launch their mainland Italian assault and chose 3 September to land Montgomery's desert veterans of the Eighth Army at Reggio, with 1st Parachute Division landing amphibiously along the coast at Tarranto. Six days later the US VIth

Corps arrived in force at Salerno. The slow and hard fought climb up the length of the Italian mainland had begun. Pietro Badoglio signed an Italian Peace agreement with Eisenhower later that summer leaving the German Army to fight on in Southern Italy alone. 5th Army took Naples on 1 October and Montgomery's 8th took Foggia to the same schedule. Italy declared war on Germany during the 13 October and increased severity in fighting took place around the Gustav Line south of Rome. With worsening winter weather the assault slowed and it was not until January 1944 that a renewed assault took on the hilltop redoubt at Monte Cassino along with additional landings which took place at Anzio in attempts to cut communication lines and force withdrawal of the German 10th Army. German resistance finally cracked in the area during Spring and Rome fell on 5 June 1944. With the German 10th Army now pursued further north and fighting strong defensive actions all the way into winter the combat again ground to a halt as the snow and chilling temperatures took effect in the Northern mountains. Spring 1945 saw the seasonally effected campaign resume once again, until a treaty of unconditional surrender was signed in May at Casserta by General Karl Wolff. Fighting halted everywhere in Italy two days later when General Heinrich Vietinghoff, Commander of all German Forces in the country agreed and signed to the same terms. The Shermans shown operating with British, Canadian and New Zealand Armoured units in this chapter largely resemble those seen in North Africa, because initially at the beginning of the campaign they were largely the same tanks repainted. As the campaign progresses the arrival of the Firefly model and later production types is recorded. This is the Sherman tank as it looked in Italy.

Intensive exercises were held along the North African coast throughout June of 1943. Difficult beach landing areas were chosen to test the durability of tracks on volcanic surfaces for Sicily would be their next destination. Here an M4 Sherman is backed onto an LCT during training. IWM NA 3513

(6 June 1943) Comparison of two tanks side by side on Sicillian Coast, Sexton 25-pounder described as a Priest in original caption which was built on Sherman Chassis in the background leave landing craft to move inland on exercise. The M4 tank on the left has periscope for driver only and direct vision slots fitted and on the right an M4A2 with headlights and siren fitted. This variant also has the early direct vision slots fitted signalling early production run. IWM NA 3511

Sherman M4A2 tank is loaded onto an LCT on 6 June 1943 where valuable lessons for the Normandy Invasion were learnt. No rear turret box is fitted to this tank, which was a usual British service addition. IWM NA 3514

Beckoned off the landing craft, this exercise improved the speedy loading/unloading of armour with a guide external to the tank who provided hand signals. It appears to be an early M4A2. IWM NA 3516

Rumbling out of the dockside area after a comparatively easy landing in Sicily during July 1943, this 6th Armoured Division M4 advances inland. IWM NA 3550

Reversed on so these M4A2's can be driven off forward facing on arrival, the jokers harbourside have written slogans and good luck phrases onto the dust-caked wading funnels. (July 1943) 'Get it while it's 'ot!' is one slogan on the lead tank. IWM NA 3955

July 1943 and Highland Division Infantry and Armour are landed – 'Sun Shield' framework to erect camo netting and canvas 'artificial lorry' cover can be seen mounted on this M4A2 Sherman, note the use of British Infantry style helmets hanging from turret and bomb thrower mounted on turret. Sun Shield was later renamed and evolved into the 'House Boat' scheme in the UK before D-Day and operated on a similar line of erecting a large canvas disguise over the tank to fool air reconnaissance sorties. IWM NA 4197

Loading between 3-10 July, these Shermans are from 50th R.T.R and are Sicily bound, many have 2" bomb throwers fitted to turrets.
IWM NA 4160

Taken between 3-10 July, more M4 and M4A2 Shermans aboard this Sicily bound LCT. Note the differences around driver's hoods with casting versus welded hood, and direct vision slots fitted to the tank on the right. IWM NA 4162

The full load in place on one LCT. Wading trunks and British infantry style helmets are visible as these Shermans are loaded ready for landing on Sicily. More bomb throwers are visible on these M4A2 variants. IWM NA 4166

Clive, a rounded single cast transmission cover M4A2 lands in Sicily. The original caption only notes that 'LCT 367 carried out its task, as tanks come ashore.' Additional fuel and oil is racked onto the hull as are ammunition crates. Look at the camo scheme too.
IWM NA 4264

Taken 10 July 1943, a good example of Siscilian Invasion camo scheme, this Sherman exhibits three colour scheme, with a sprayed on divider line, and also retains frame work fitting for Sun Shade used in the desert. Everything is in place to go into immediate action!
IWM NA 4188

11 July, 1943. 'CHU' moving inland from 'George Beach' in pursuit of the enemy with the remains of wading trunk still in place, this Sherman heads down the road while commander keeps an eye out for enemy aircraft over head. (Taken by Sgt Chetwyn, AFPU)
IWM NA 4369a

15 July 1943 and success is being well established on the advance through the Island. A Sherman M4A2 of 44th RTR being passed by Austin K2 Ambulance , note caked dust and the holed damage to front wing. The story behind the crew of this particular tank is told in NA4531's caption.
IWM NA 4532

Taken by Sgt Mott on 15 July 1943, this photo shows some of the British Sherman crews of 44th RTR who captured the Commander of the Napolli Division General Gotti-Porcinari and his Headquarters Staff. Shortly after this photograph was taken the crews were ordered to mount up and continue to Carlintini after the RAF had bombed. Note the sand-shield wing has been punctured twice on front right side. IWM NA 4531

12 July 1943. Narrow roads and crumbling track were hazards to be overcome for the Sherman driver in the Med. Here a Sherman M4A2 has rolled down a small incline off the road. Note jeep's unusual camo pattern in the background. The road apparently collapsed in the dry heat under the weight of the tank and here crewmen and recovery experts ponder the task ahead. IWM NA 4550

10 July and Sgt. Silverside (AFPU) travelling with troops through Cassible on Sicily captures this shot as an M4 Sherman rolls through the huge masonry gateway to the town. Note the markings obscured by dust coating , an early armoured forces tricolour painted on turret side. The early direct vision slots and three piece transmission cover identify this as an early M4 production model.
IWM NA 4581

Sgt. Rooke, AFPU snaps another photographer at work as he focuses on a passing Sherman M4A2, 12 July 1943. IWM NA 4649

Condor creates a dust storm on 4 August, 1943 advancing across the Catania Plain before reaching the hills around Paterno. A smoke discharger bracket is fitted to the turret on this M4. IWM NA 5522

5 August, 1943 entering Catania an M4A2 Sherman and deserted local tram vie for space down the Via Garibaldi. This tank belonged to 44 RTR and was cheered into the city by Sicilian civilians. It is still marked up LST 3/6 from the landing and has the rounded one piece cast transmission cover fitted. British style 'wing bins' are fitted to the front of the tank. IWM NA 5558

Local Sicilian children enjoy the arrival of M4A2 'RAJPUT' as tanks park up in Catanian streets. Rear deck equipment includes camo netting, ammo boxes and even the mugs for a quick brew! (5 August, 1943.) IWM NA 5561

The Fall of Regalbuto on 5 August 1943. Rubble strewn streets are no obstacle to this dust covered Canadian Sherman M4 although one pictures the imagery of the dust created by a column of tanks moving at speed and how this would easily betray numbers, direction and intentions. Royal Engineers had already filled the craters in the bombed streets before the Canadians arrived twenty-four hours later and even the BBC reported that the town had been taken by Canadian Forces. In fact the Devons had assaulted the outer defences and the Dorsets and Royal Engineers were first to enter the town and pacify enemy resistance. IWM NA 5593

Submerged in foliage, this Sherman let's rip with its main gun as an infantry observer looks on. The blade sight protrudes from the camouflage. IWM NA 5786

Landing Craft loading detail daubed across transmission cover, this Sherman M4 crew meet local villagers in Reggio. General Montgomery had observed the landings at close quarters at Reggio and had recently passed along the same road. The local inhabitants remained to cheer on the rest of the liberating force. IWM NA 6223

Dusty Canadian Sherman crews of the 1st Canadian Division check maps in Reggio during September, 1943. Note the double smoke dischargers fitted to the turret and good view afforded of the rounded steel cuff track, type T54E2. IWM NA 6241

M4 advancing onto the Italian mainland. 'War Admiral' the famous American race horse has provided inspiration for the naming of this tank. Pistol port is open and penant flies. Infantry are caked in dust from the traffic as usual on the road near Mileto. They race up country in pursuit of the retreating enemy. (17 September, 1943) IWM NA 6560

1C Hybrid version of the Firefly type Sherman mounted with 17-pounder AT gun, (note cast front to hull) using cover amongst buildings in preparation for firing on enemy strong-points on the banks of the River Reno in Italy on 6 April 1945. It was about to fire in support of C Company, 1st Btn, London Irish Rifles making an assault crossing. The Firefly model is illustrated in all its guises throughout the chapters in this book. It remained the most powerful version of the Sherman in British service during the Second World War. Unusual track extensions made from 'T' section angle iron are fitted to rubber chevron tracks, and logs are roped to the sides of the hull. Camo net, bedrolls and tarps are strapped on the rear of the deck and rear of turret displays a large squadron identification sign and additional stowage box as seen on many Shermans in Italy. IWM NA 23754

A frontal view of the same 1C Hybrid rolling into position. T-shaped track extensions and welded ammunition boxes on the front glacis plate have been utilised, a common British adaptation, to provide more external storage of personal kit. War Office designed camo pattern for the gun barrel is present. This particular scheme was specific to the 17-pounder main gun barrel on Allied tanks, and involved counter shading with white paint both inside the muzzle brake and along the underside of the barrel to the point on the barrel where the regular 75mm gun barrel would end. The idea, and effective it was, was to give the impression from observation at a distance that the tank was only fitted with standard armament. See various other examples of this W/O Counter-Shading scheme in Chapters 6 and 7. IWM NA 23755

Three point turn being conducted on narrow dusty track in order to squeeze between these farm buildings and use them as cover on the top bank of the River Senio. Note large number painted on appliqué armour patch and the destruction of the un-mettled road due to the tank. This tank of C Squadron, 18 Armoured Regiment was being used in support of the 2nd New Zealand Division along the banks of the river. Fascine carriers and bridging tanks appear in the same series in preparation for the assault crossing. IWM NA 23797

Over the River Santerno on 12 April 1945. This heavily camouflaged Sherman is probably a 1C Hybrid although it is difficult to tell in this 'mobile bush' incarnation. A tin can has been placed half way up the barrel, and W/O counter-shaded camouflage paint scheme with hessian wrapping used on barrel end disguises its true power from enemy observation. T-shaped track extenders are again apparent. Note the crewman sat in the additional loaders hatch cut into the top of the turret, another method of identifying Firefly of 105mm howitzer turreted variants. IWM NA 24026

North of Imola on 17 April 1945 a New Zealand 4th Armoured Brigade Hybrid 1C Firefly travelling at max speed through the town of Medicina. This town was heavily fortified by the Germans, with earthworks thrown up to block every street and anti-tank weapons stockpiled. However, not a shot was fired in the liberation of the town due to the sheer speed of allied advance. Note the counter-shaded barrel end. The three bogies have been turned white by the caking of dust! The cast and welded composition hull is clearly outlined IWM NA 24147

In the devastated streets of Portomaggiore, men of the 5th Northants, (56 British Division) take a pause in the advance. Stretcher bearers pass a Sherman mounted with single smoke discharger. A knocked out Tiger tank which had been backed into a collapsing building had been assaulted by Infantry to provide safe passage for this armour. The road from Portomaggiore led onwards to Argenta with further unknown dangers ahead. This early M4 has a .30 MG to use for AA cover and has British type T51 Cast steel track, plus appliqué armour added to the turret cheek.
IWM NA 24246

Near Ferrara, Infantry of the Lancashire Fusiliers, 11 Bde, 78th British Division move forward partnering M4A2 Sherman armour on 20 April 1945. IWM NA 24365

Chapter Six

NW Europe –
Normandy to Belgium & Holland

After the amphibious Normandy assault on 6 June it was apparent that a stalemate would ensue inland unless the breakout of Allied forces was achieved quickly. Armour had to reach the beach first, and stay ashore implementing one of the major lessons from the Dieppe Raid of 1942. Clearly the armour required not only flotation aids, but also means of propulsion enabling them to spread out and avoid presenting a concentrated target while coming ashore. One experimental device that had been tested and proven was that fitted to a British Valentine Tank of the series originally considered to spearhead the assault on D-Day as far back as early 1943. However just as successful results on the Valentine DD tests were being tabulated the entire breadth of work on specialized spearhead armour (The Funnies) was being handed over to Major General P C S Hobart, at 79th Armoured Division in the UK who was a distant relative of Bernard Law Montgomery. Under Hobart's direction he insisted that the Straussler Flotation Kit which had been so promising in tests, invented by a Mr Nicholas Straussler be fitted to first line Sherman Tanks as he knew the Valentine already to be obsolete.

Testing showed that the water displacement required for a 40-ton tank to float could be created by a collapsible rubberized canvas folding screen, mounted on a mild steelplatform around the standard hull if waterproofed well at the line the armour met the sand shields. Some of the photographs in the Normandy series demonstrate these screens, the thin steel platform and the rubberized canvas in raised and lowered positions. The screen was erected in the landing craft by inflating 36 tubular rubber pillars with compressed air, and as an additional support thirteen steel pillars locked it inplace in case of damage. The circumference of the screen was protected by three tubular steel frames which provided support against external water pressure from the sea. Once on the beach the floating tank could lower the screen and operate as a regular turret tank. Propulsion was dealt with by employing two 26-inch diametre propellers which ran off a bevel gear and pinion connection to the drive rotating the tracks. These propellers were disengaged and swung upwards out of the way when the tank was on the land to provide clearance for road or cross country travel. A small bilge pump was even fitted to remove ingressed water from the top of the Hull and from inside the vehicle. Lastly the steering had be addressed, and it was – by attaching a small platform to the rear of the hull the commander of each DD tank could stand overlooking the screen and control the direction with a hand operated tiller paddle.

General Eisenhower was impressed by a demonstration of these Duplex Drive (DD)Tanks in January 1944 and it was earmarked for Canadian, British and American use on 6 June. Hobart's limited production facilities were unable to convert enough in the timescale so plans plus a DD expert were flown over to America the day following the demonstration resulting in a hundred American DD tanks arriving into Liverpool Dock within six weeks. As a rule, British conversions used M4A2 and M4A4 types and the later American converted DD's were built on basic M4 and M4A1 variants. When the moment of truth arrived the DD faired well on D-Day for the British and Canadian forces who landed all of their tanks and got nearly all of them off the shoreline. However the American force of 29 DD's experienced a loss of 27 in the water due to launching against the flow of the tide and at a greater distance from shore. Recent archeological work on the sea bed off the coast has located nearly all of the lost American DD tanks. Their success on British sectors however ensured their use in the Rhine Crossing of March 1945, and on the Elbe River crossing operation of April 1945. To achieve advancement inland from the beachheads there were going to be some large battles. Allied commanders knew this, and planned for them. German armour and re-enforcements had been rushed to the Normandy Front the moment they could be released from other duties, or had orders finally authorised and a face-off of proportion was imminent. Allied Forces were pouring from the beaches while German troops were being rushed to Normandy from the interior. Montgomery always claimed after the war that the Normandy Campaign had unfolded exactly as he had planned it, but this notion has been debated from the moment he made the claim I feel. Many factors demonstrate the reality was quite different. There were some serious problems with the advance into France shortly after 6 June as was demonstrated by the inexperienced British Commanders and formations at Villers Bocage among other face to face encounters with the enemy.

Villers Bocage was a demonstration of all that was inexperienced with British armoured force application at the beginning of the Normandy Campaign. Long spread out columns of tanks, light recce tanks to the front followed on by support vehicles and at the very rear the lorried infantry that should have been on call to protect the precious force. Stopping to celebrate with French villagers, a party atmosphere took over before the column began to advance up the single road which gently rose to the next way point. Michael Wittman, tank ace from Russian front experience, with other tanks of his unit were in position and waiting. Carnage and chaos followed in what has become one of the most infamous of armoured actions in the Second World War. Travelling in the opposite direction to the single British column Wittman was able to rumble down the entire column inside his 88mm armed Tiger, shooting at will, taking life and destroying machinery.

Monty's scheme to kickstart the larger breakout, and avoid similar experience was formulated in Operation EPSOM and GOODWOOD. Hundreds of Allied Shermans with other armour, massed across the Orne Canal to move on Caen in the hope that all German armoured forces would counterattack and be drawn north to meet them. A pathway would be created for the American Forces in Southern Normandy to crack on with the breakout, pulling around to the North of Caen at speed and enveloping the German Forces. With the enemy totally destroyed in the Normandy region, Paris would be the next obtainable objective. From Paris the leapfrogging to Berlin would continue. GOODWOOD was abandoned however on 20 July after 11th Armoured Division lost some 400 tanks on the ground known as the Borguebus Ridge where they faced some of the best prepared defences the Axis created anywhere in the Second World War. GOODWOOD was not a total failure, it did expand the bridgehead seven miles inland and coupled with the Canadian Corps action 'Atlantic' achieved the clearing of Caen of German resistance.

Operation BLUECOAT, the breakout from Caumont eventually cracked the German resolve which became full-flight in attempts to escape around Falaise. After the collapse of German resistance at Falaise, and elation to be free of the Bocage countryside, huge advances were made by the British toward the Belgian border leaving only the long supply routes and rear camps in France. A distance of some 250 miles was covered in three weeks, and in particular the Irish Guards were able to motor ninety-seven miles in just twelve hours – one of the fastest advances in contemporary military history. An optimistic mood swept the Allied forces, a feeling that perhaps German resistance had been cracked by this total rout. This mood was prevalent across the breadth of the Allied Command structure, and lead to the floating of a new plan: MARKET GARDEN. In the late summer of 1944, Montgomery persuaded General Dwight D Eisenhower with a scheme that intended to capitalize on the German retreat and bring the war to a close by year end. The plan proposed a combined Allied airborne force dropping behind German lines in a lightning strike to capture crossing points over the Rhine. To consolidate he would push a vast ground force up a single road in support, and to help hold the crossing points (Bridges) until further troops could cross over the river and to strengthen the bridgeheads. The route to the Industrial Ruhr and heartland of the German war machine would be shortened, and control attained in the success of his noble suggestion.

'Market Garden' , Monty's ambitious battle-plan very nearly succeeded. 'Market', the airborne phase was an enormous operation alone. Some 5,000 fighters, bombers and transport aircraft, towing more than 2,500 gliders. All were packed full of ammunition, vehicles, equipment and troops – their contents amounted to an entire Allied Airborne Army. The land based support for this air armada was massed on the Dutch-Belgian border. The 'Garden' forces were forming up for the dash to the bridges and XXX Corps' Armoured formations were massed for the kick-off on 17 September when both components of Market Garden would go into action with the airborne forces preceding the ground by just an hour and five minutes.

We now know the form the battle took as the lightly armed airborne force found itself landing in an area heavily populated by the 2nd SS *Panzer* Corps. XXX Corps fought a slow and often delayed approach along the single road earmarked for the relief force and a bitter battle ensued. *Panzerfaust, Nebelwerfer* and Anti-tank guns flanked the road for most of the route. Parts of Arnhem town were completely levelled in the fighting, and the British evacuated the town on the night of 26 September, nine days after arriving. The 1st Airborne Division would never recover from the losses sustained during the battle, and it should be noted that the Allied armies took more casualties on this operation than they had assaulting the shore on D-Day. Airborne and Ground Force casualties combined to produce a figure of some 17,000 men. The British had to accept 13,226. Horrock's XXX Corps were missing 1,480 and the 8th and 12th Corps an additional 3,874. German figures remain unknown but estimates touch 10,000 troops from Army Group B and up to a quarter of these may have been killed. Dutch civilian casualties were relatively light considering the fighting was taking place in the houses of the local populace – they were recorded as low at the time but figures are not known for sure. The US Forces also lost nearly 8,000 men including aircrew in wounded, dead and missing during the battle.

By 27 September 1944 Eisenhower knew Germany would have to be taken inch by inch, by troops on the ground and that the retreat exhibited by the Germans in Normandy had been turned around. They had certainly not lost any will in the fight, and would be a potentially even more dangerous foe when time came to defend their homeland. Fighting slowed in the winter of 1944 due to biting cold and heavy snowfall in one of the worst weather spells in recorded European history. On the 16 December the German High Command launched an attempt to reverse the direction of the European war in the Ardennes. During the 'Von Runstedt Offensive' or 'Battle of The Bulge' they intended to cross the River Meuse, retake Antwerp and isolate the British Army from the Americans. Montgomery was temporarily given command responsibility to repel the German advance in the north using 21st Army Group Forces, while Bradley would command US Forces. Monty ordered Lt. Gen

Brian Horrocks and his XXX Corps to leave Holland immediately and swing toward the combat zone in order to occupy defensive positions between Givet and Maastricht, stopping the advancing Germans from crossing the Meuse. On 22 December the 51st Highland and 53rd Welsh Divisions and 29th and 33rd Armoured Brigades with the 43rd Wessex Division in the reserve arrived. Also 6th Airborne paratroopers were trucked to the area between Dinant and Marche-en-Famenne as bad weather prohibited a drop by aircraft. Fighting continued throughout the Christmas period with Shermans of RTR engaged in clashes against armour from 2nd *Panzer*. The Allied counter-offensive began on 3 January 1945 and by 8 January, the Germans were being ordered to withdraw from the Bulge and retreat. It was over by 16 January, when Montgomery decided to move XXX Corps to the Netherlands again for a refit and preparation for the planned offensive thrust across the Rhine: This is how the Sherman looked during the advance from Normandy into Belgium and Holland to the point of preparations for the Rhine crossings in March of 1945.

Making the Channel crossing, wading funnels and large turret numbers visible. This photograph taken by Sgt Mapham, AFPU, on the morning of 6 June 1944 provides a view of an LST upper deck loaded with tanks and men from 13th/18th Hussars (27th Beach Brigade) about a mile offshore from Hermanville Sur Mer. M4 or M4A4 'BALACLAVA' and in front a strengthened turret of an ARV, note also the Despatch rider hitching a ride with his bike. IWM B 5110

This M4A4 fought with the 3rd Division approaching Lion-Sur-Mer on 6 June squeezing alongside a DUKW, note numbers on rear turret stowage box as well as either side of turret. IWM B 5025

Skirts lowered these DD (Duplex Drive Amphibious) Tanks move inland with commando teams from 1st Special Service Brigade to clear the roadways out of the immediate beach areas and to consolidate the Glider Forces who had been holding territory against counter-attack since 12.30am on 6 June. Troops stay in contact using a portable wireless transceiver at the roadside. IWM B 5055

Crab flail Sherman which also floundered on the beach. Note 79th Armoured Division badge to left of roller. It actually belonged to the Westminster Dragoons and came to grief during the landings. Barrage balloons now fill the sky in the background providing air protection to the fleet. IWM B 5141

Abandoned DD tank on the invasion beach, it's skirt has collapsed and has been ripped away by tidal flow as men of the 13th/18th Hussars stop to survey the scene on the landing beach. IWM B 5190

DD tanks of 27th Armoured Brigade reach Airborne Forces and complete the link up with the Seaborne troops. Taken on 10 June 1944 by Sgt Christie as he came across these Paratroops of 12th Parachute Battalion. They help to extinguish a fire on the skirt of DD tank after a sharp engagement on the landing grounds near Ranville. The DD tanks had used the cover of the Gliders spread about to engage the enemy who counter-attacked to cut the Ranville Road and in an attempt to seize the Caen Bridges. The paratroopers had been fighting a guerilla style war against the Wehrmacht for three days before heavier firepower from the beaches arrived! IWM B 5347

11 June 1944. Typical Normandy crossroads near Bayeux where an M4A4 advances along with men of A Company, Durham Light Infantry of the 50th Division. IWM B 5379

VC Firefly travelling up from the beaches on 10 June 1944. Turret is reversed and barrel protected in the gun crutch. The base of the wading trunk for exhaust expulsion remains at the rear. The Sherman V rear stowage box has been removed and probably refitted to the front hull to allow space for the wading gear before in the invasion. Unloaded at Juno beach, this VC travels through the village of Reviers. IWM B 5385

Not every 88mm shell strike resulted in total Sherman destruction. Double pump jack is used by the crew to replace damaged road wheels splintered and deformed by the explosion – this photograph demonstrates the hard physical labour aspect of tank crew life in the field. Self sufficiency was the key until rear base workshops could safely set up in the field. These men were from C Squadron, 13th/ 18th Hussars, 27th Armoured Brigade and had been supporting Airborne Forces holding the bridge at Benouville. (10 June 1944)
IWM B 5423

Great shot of an M4A4 crew at rest in the field. Only a few days after D-Day and the white T number has already been blacked out through combat experience, no 69 on turret is still highly visible however and camo netting remains roped to the rear deck. Intercom headphones and microphone are draped within earshot of the commander. Having supported Airborne Troops at Benouville for four days without sleep they finally stand down for a few hours to rest. (taken by Sgt Mapham on 10 June, 1944)
IWM B 5425

13 June, 1944. M4 Sherman in the 50th Northumberland Division area rolls on to Tilly-Sur-Seulles on Montgomery's orders with the objective of outflanking Caen, and is seen down a typical Norman country lane. Note the degree markings painted on the exterior of the turret to assist infantry in calling in enemy positions they wanted neutralising using the BC-1362 Interphone Box mounted on the rear exterior panel of the tank. This consisted of a telephone handset with access to the commander's intercom inside the vehicle – infantry could literally make a call in to request direct fire support. The gunners inside would be working to the same indication and parity in sighting the main gun was achieved. Centaur tanks follow on. IWM B 5454

Sherman VC Firefly of 14 Platoon, 1st Battalion, South Lancashires, with no attempt made by the crew to camouflage the length of the 17-pounder barrel confidently sitting out in No-Man's Land. Rear panel stowage box has been moved to front hull to allow for wading funnels. The counterweight and turret stowage box can be seen from this angle at the rear of turret. (13 June 1944) IWM B 5546

BARV at work on 14 June 1944 towing a jeep through the surf, snapped by AFPU man Sgt Morris. BARV Commander protrudes from top hatch, microphone in hand. IWM B 5579

Pushing inland – Bren Carriers and Infantry of The Seaforth Highlanders intermingled with Shermans in this column advancing inland on the Vassy Road. Note spare track on the front hull of this Sherman and white ID star painted on the spare wheel carried on the hull of the lead Bren carrier. (4 August 1944) IWM B 8601

7th Armoured Division M4 knocked out in previous battle at Villers Bocage. Salvage Crews have already removed the main gun, but the tank will be towed away and rebuilt in a field workshop. The ferocity of this engagement is given away by the state of the village around the tank even though this photograph was taken weeks after the battle on 5 August by Sgt Mapham. The town is completely destroyed and in ruins after street fighting, aerial and artillery bombardment by both sides. The main advance had by passed the town and it was the job of the Royal Engineers to make the streets clear and safe from booby traps and mines left by the enemy. IWM B 8632

Hybrid IC drives past Sgt Midgley, AFPU, in the chase after the enemy through Briquessard and Aunay-Sur-Odon. Summer heat and the heavy transport has turned the roads and tracks into dust. IWM B 8675

A BBC French reporter records the sound of a VC Firefly as it rumbles past at speed creating clouds of dust during the advance in August, 1944. He utilised a small transmitter built in a local building which would send his reports back to London for vetting and editing. They would then be re-broadcast in his native French language to listeners in France. IWM B 8710

6 August, 1944. A DD tank with remains of metal support network at the front of the tank has run through a hedgerow and misjudged the drop on the other side. Here recovery teams attempt to pull it out of the ditch which was located just behind the lines. The original caption records that 'this tank would be put back into action as no task was too difficult for the recovery teams!' IWM B 8741

Sharing out the rations before the attack south of Caen in front of HELMDON, an M4A4 on 7 August. IWM B 8796

Australian Officer briefs his crew next to 'Lillingstone' an M4A4 in preparation for the attack on Caen. Troop Commander Lt E H Brown of Queensland, Australia gives operational codes and orders to other tank commanders (l to r) Cpl S Upstone of Brackley, Lt E H Brown, L/Cpl A W Dwight of Whitchurch and Cpl Sumner of Sheffield. IWM B 8798

8 August, 1944. Polish Armoured troops before the advance on Caen have been directed to this staging area near their start line by Military Police. Here last minute adjustments are made and checked. Note white recognition stars and T numbers now blacked out. The Polish tanks supported the advance of 51st Highland Division during the attack. IWM B 8823

Polish Firefly, possibly a Hybrid IC on the start line, 8 August 1944. Barrel is wound in rope in an alternative attempt to disguise its silhouette. IWM B 8826

Driver adjusts the rear view mirror on this Sherman, (rarely fitted in combat) leading a long column that has pulled up awaiting Op Goodwood to kick off. Scammell recovery truck is poised at the front of the column and one receives a clear understanding of the scale of this armoured advance. IWM B 8830

A row of Sherman Crabs await flailing duty to clear minefields before infantry and armour advance from 7th Armoured Division south of Aunay-Sur-Odon. These flails headed the column and are about to move on Plessis-Grimoult, on the southern slopes of Mont Pincon. IWM B 8844

9 August 1944. Tank recovery and repair units kept close behind the lines to repair tanks damaged in action. Tanks were quickly repaired and put back into action by REME Craftsmen. Here men of an 8th Armoured Brigade w/shop are seen replacing a radial engine with new crated spare just behind the front line on an M4A1 cast hull. IWM B 8892

In the 8th Armoured Brigade workshops, August, 1944. A distinctive 'egg shaped' 17-pounder muzzle-brake is replaced on one Firefly barrel by S/Sgt F Hunt of Burgess Hill, Sussex and Cfn Shannan of Reading. This barrel has not been painted with the W/O Counter-Shaded scheme. IWM B 8894

Sherman ARV tows a disabled tank through the ruined village of Bourgebus in August of 44. The recovery crew happily sit on top of the ARV and smoke as they pass the wrecked church on their way to a Field Repair Workshop. IWM B 8910

Taken on 13 August by Sgt. Gee, AFPU, battle damaged broken vehicles are recovered to a repair centre. Scammel and trailer bring in a trackless Sherman for urgent attention. IWM B 9091

The M4 tank is checked in with the Workshop Repair Office and recovery crew report to the Officer in charge. IWM B 9092

The Scammel driver operates the winch from his cab which slowly releases this trackless Sherman down the trailer so that repairs can get underway. IWM B 9093

REME Officer discusses the work order and inspects damage. He also carries out an assessment of usuable parts. IWM B 9094

Brigadier 'Pip' Roberts (right), Commanding Officer 11th Armoured Division meets a fellow officer holding ply box lid in use as temporary map board next to 'Kay' his personal early version M4A4 Command Tank in the Bocage of Normandy. His tank features additional aerial mounting on the front hull slope, as well as aerial mounted on turret. A white Allied recognition encircled star is visible on the top of the turret. Note the machine gun shield on the right of turret gun mount, and crew kit attached to turret due to confined internal space.

Improvised wadding has been used in the barrel to seal it from debris as it rolled into these concealed positions. 11th Armoured Divisional bull on yellow background insignia is apparent on the left side of the three piece transmission cover and the '50' indicates a Brigade HQ vehicle painted on right. T54E2 type steel tracks are fitted, notable by the rounded edges of the track block cuffs and absence of three large round headed rivets which kept the two halves of the track blocks together on the T62 track. IWM B 9184

Sherman M4A4 leads a column of Guards Armoured Division tanks through the village of Thilliers. Note that German helmets have been fitted over the headlights to afford some lens protection, additional T62 track segments are affixed to boost frontal armour and air raid siren is still mounted to front driver's side wing not often retained on British Shermans. The wet and muddy conditions have obliterated all allied marking. (31 August 1944) IWM BU 288

Sherman VC of the Guards Armoured Division cross country near Les Thilliers, to the west of Beauvais. Note the workshop scratch-built gun crutch, additional extra track armour and road wheel mounted on the front plate. The 17-pounder barrel appears neither wrapped in hessian camo strips or War Office camouflage scheme painted. This photo provides an excellent view of one version of the armour plug welded hull .30 MG modification. The crew position was deleted to allow for extra ammunition stowage. This is potentially the first item other than the barrel to examine when determining Fireflies in original photography. IWM BU 298

FFI (French Resistance Fighters) chalk messages of goodwill on the sides of passing M4A2 Sherman column. Note the bomb thrower mounted in the commander's turret hatch, British adaptation of tool box mounted on rear panel, and stowage bin mounted on the rear of the turret. An additional container has been strapped on to the bin. IWM BU 303

Dead horses and discarded German steel helmets litter this country road near Arras. Another Cullin device fitted to the lead tank, which has also utilised plenty of spare track to protect the driver's area. IWM BU 261

Guards Armoured Shermans advance passed a WWI memorial on the The Somme at the hilltop which overlooks Fouilloy. A Sherman VC with hessian wrapped barrel overtakes another in the stationary column. Welded hull MG ports can be seen on both tanks, while the M4A4 in the front is fitted with the American designed Culin hedgerow device. Rarely are British Shermans seen with this fitting which is detailed in the American Service Chapter elsewhere in this book. Note other than divisional insignia all allied recognition stars have been painted over or removed entirely by this crew. A large white star provides an appealing targetting aid to anti-tank gunners! IWM BU 269

Churchill track sections are applied to the outer hull by this experienced crew as they also pass a First World War memorial on the Somme. Siren remains intact on the front wing and allied stars have been painted over along the side of the hull. The aerial from the turret has been 'hoop painted' in contrasting black and white to break its outline up. The additional loader's hatch in the Firefly behind it is in use demonstrating the improved access to the turret areas when 17-pounder was fitted . Kit bags are stowed on the rear engine deck out of the crews' working space. IWM BU 272

M10 Tank destroyers parked up in a Brussels square are met by a column of Shermans as the crowds turn out to celebrate. The liberated people of Brussels gave the British tanks a tremendous welcome! IWM BU 506

The populace of Brussels celebrating Liberation after a four year wait. Some twenty-five civilians crowd onto this heavily camouflaged British Sherman. Note the board on the front lower hull which aided equipment storage. IWM BU 508

The reality of daily advances toward the Fatherland. Here British tanks cross the Albert Canal at Berringnen. The original bridge had been blown by the Germans and had been repaired by the British under fire. Dutch soldiers of the Princess Irene Regiment captured the bridge and held it. In this photo the recently taken bridge and approach road is protected by 17-pounder Anti-Tank Gun, and infantrymen (one armed with captured Mauser K98K Rifle.) The Sherman M4A4 is then waved on carrying spare road wheels mounted on the hull. Netting has been used to break up the outline of the hull, and slogans have been chalked along the side of the hull in morale boosting efforts. The troops in the foxhole are (from left) Irish Guards and Princess Irene Regiment (right.) IWM BU 719

A rare sight in picture reference books, but a common one for tanks crews during the war. The dead commander of an M4A4 (note the bar grill cover behind the turret where hull was extended to accommodate the A57 Multibank engine) lays slumped over the rear stowage box of his turret. Passing troops on the road to Eindhoven have laid a Great Coat over his body, but the severity of his head wound suggests there was no possibility of saving this life. Either a shell splinter or sniper had found its target silhouetted high in the turret, against a clear sky. (18 September 1944.) IWM BU 927

XXX Corps on the road to Eindhoven, stop briefly to chat with cheering crowds in the town of Valkenswaard the day after the enormous Airborne Force drop on Arnhem and surrounding areas. Note the rear stowage box attached to the rear of the hull on the M4A4 to the right. The First Aid Box has been moved to the far left of the rear panel, and a reel of telephone cabling attached to the right. (18 September 1944.) IWM BU 931

British tanks enter Eindhoven on 19 September. This photo snapped by Captain Malindine, AFPU, shows the liberated crowds flocking around XXX Corps vehicles as they pass through the town. Stowage boxes have been moved to the front. IWM BU 936

Infantryman watches as a Sherman speeds into Asten having crossed the Bois Le Duc Canal at Zomeren. The censor has obliterated tunic badges. (22 September 1944.)
IWM BU 1084

Loading up an M4A4 with ammo before the Rhine Crossing operation in February 1945. Note track extenders used and camouflage attached to front glacis plate. T Number is still visible. The road led down to the banks of the Rhine.
IWM BU 1966

Chapter Seven

NW Europe – Spring 1945 into Germany and Victory

By the Spring of 1945 the Allies are pushing well into Germany. Large scale tank to tank confrontations had become highly unlikely as much of the larger German armour, vulnerable when operating in the field without its logistical support networks, had already been destroyed in Normandy, and in Belgium. Massive armoured, air and manpower were pitted against the millions of remaining German troops and civilians still motivated to defend the homeland. Anti-tank guns and the hand held rocket launcher became the most feared weapon at the opposition's disposal. Although soon to become homeless, with infrastructure smashed , equipment destroyed and their capital city occupied in ruins but there was fight left in the German soldier yet. In March, Hitler had ordered all bridges on the Rhine be destroyed after additional assaults threatened the Ruhr after the failure of MARKET GARDEN. His plan was to leave not one left standing of the road and rail crossings that existed along the banks of the river. However, one did remain when demolition charges failed to bring it down on a single attempt. This crossing was the Ludendorff Railway Bridge at Remagen in Southern Germany. In the last days of the Reich, Hitler had the officers responsible executed. Goerring called for Air Force volunteers to crash their jet aircraft into it, but Hodges had already pushed nearly 8,000 troops over from 9th US Armoured Division, and the 78th Infantry Division. They fanned out on the other side after crossing and secured a bridgehead six miles in, framed between the bridge and the Cologne-Frankfurt Autobahn.

The forging of the bridgehead lead to some controversy between British and US Commanders. One plan had Montgomery and 21st Army Group crossing the Dutch border in the North and taking a north-westerly route fighting across the open plains of Germany. Eisenhower was not as easily swayed as he found himself to be pre-MARKET GARDEN and decided on delivering his main assault elsewhere. Hodges had made the crossing and secured the bridgehead and so it was felt it was his duty to push on inland. The main thrust would continue over the Remagen bridge and the US First Army would drive on Marburg at rapid pace. Patton's 3rd

Army crossed the Rhine lower down the river at Oppenheim and drove up the country in a north-easterly direction so as to link up with Hodges just a few days later.

Opposition in the East of Germany was weak, and crumbling every day with the threat of the Red Army's advances. Kesselring supposedly had sixty divisions at his disposal on paper but the reality on the battlefield numbered a fraction of that force. Many townsfolk were quick to assist the Allied advance, once a few shells had been sent into the outskirts of their villages and towns. Prisoners were also being taken in large numbers, revealing the desperation of the *Whermacht* in trawls which showed the retired, and the children were now being called into the ranks. Eisenhower's plan was for US forces to push on eastwards slicing Germany in two while the British skirted the northern slice passing through the ports and industrial centres along the coast. The US forces would head for the remaining central industrialised areas around Leipzig and Dresden. Patch's 7th US Army and the French would head on a southerly route. By 18 April 1945 the last German forces inside the eighty mile Ruhr Pocket had surrendered. Surrounded on all sides, 317,000 soldiers were taken prisoner and vast swathes of equipment lay destroyed or in Allied hands. This was a higher prisoner count than at either Stalingrad, or at the close of fighting in Tunisia. The fight within the German population had been all but extinguished.

Near Duisberg, after the Ruhr Pocket surrender, German General Walter Model walked into the woods and shot himself. The last days of the Reich had arrived. Hodges army was motoring at speed across Central Germany and linked up with 3rd Army. All along the route they were now being met only with white bed sheets and flags hung in every town square. Resistance became extremely sporadic, as it did for the British in the north, who were mainly confronting small groups of Volksturm or Hitler Jugend units mixed with die-hard *Kampfgruppe*'s here and there on the roads to Berlin. The speed and numbers involved in the allied advance though rendered it impossible to stop. The River Elbe had been crossed by DD Shermans in April, but troops were halted there. Roosevelt had preordained that it would be the Russians who entered Berlin first. Magdeburg, where US forces were halted was just a short drive from the city limits but they were held at this position. The US First Army fought on past Leipzig and reached the Elbe lower down at Dessau, managing to liberate the POW's of Colditz en route. The Red Army was racing westward and pushing a desperate number of Germans ahead of it as they ran hoping to be captured by the British or Americans in preference.

On 25 April, days before Hitler was to end his life in the Berlin bunker HQ he had retreated to, the Americans and Russians met up – twice. Once initially and secondly in a staged version for the motion picture and stills cameramen in a reconstruction at Torgau. Two and a quarter million German prisoners had been captured since D-Day. During May, Montgomery at 21st Army HQ sited in a tented encampment on Luneberg Heath, took the formal surrender and the task of repairing and rebuilding Germany into a habitable state began. Days later an overall surrender document was signed at Eisenhower's HQ at Rheims. The former Reich heartland was searched for war criminals while minor politicians and town administrators were put through de-Nazification training courses.

Many of the tanks in later shots in this chapter were beginning to display their mileage, but also the experience gained by their crews. Often heavily camouflaged and protected by additional armour, Churchill tank track sections or welded on armour plate roughly cut. Here are a selection of Sherman tanks as they looked at the close of the campaign achieving the Victory in Europe:

On the 8 February 1945 a new offensive began on the Western Front involving British and Canadian troops of the First Canadian Army south-east of Nijmegan. Here a Crab flail supports infantry in the Rhine Crossing, as an upturned Waco glider provides testament to the Airborne assault that took place in the previous year. Infantry from 15th Scottish Division use the Flail tank as cover during the start of the advance. IWM BU 1693

The firing, and then sorting through ammunition casings, of a heavy barage in support of Rhine crossing by men of 15th Scottish Division, 227 Brigade, Argyll and Sutherland Highlanders in SE Nijmegan. (8 February 1945) Note the remanufactured commander's turret in IWM BU 1732 below.
IWM BU 1731 IWM BU 1732

'Operation PLUNDER'
– DD tanks used in
Rhine crossings are
directed forward by an
MP and cross into
Germany on 24 March,
1945. IWM BU 2148

Canvas skirt fully
erected, DD's emerge
from the Rhine to
cross the flood banks
built up on either side
of the river. (24 March,
1945.) IWM BU 2171

A collapsed raft drowns two Shermans mid crossing, when enemy shellfire smashed the raft pontoons. Here the recovery operation continues. Note logs and evergreen foliage on the tank in BU 2462. Luckily the tanks were close to the bank when the raft was hit and recovery operations were quick. IWM BU 2460 & BU 2462

29 March 1945 amidst the rubble of Bocholt. Heavy opposition was encountered from fanatical troops armed with MG42's and snipers had been spread around the town hidden in the detritus from collapsing buildings. This Sherman of 4th Armoured Brigade lets fly with a round straight down the road toward an enemy strongpoint, infantry would soon follow in a charge for the position. IWM BU 2774

Battle police direct a Sherman through a cross roads in the wrecked German towns of Borken and Gemen. Units of the 7th Armoured Division (Desert Rats) took the town and passed on through with rapidity. (30 March, 1945.) IWM BU 2829

7th Armoured Div
Hybrid I C Firefly
advances at speed down
a dusty road in
Stadtlohn. IWM BU 2890

Command Tank of the Coldstream Guards on 1 April 1945. Note front hull mounted additional aerial which has been hoop painted in black/white, and chicken wire used to contain grassy camo. Track extenders are fitted for extra grip. In the tank are Lieutenant Colonel RFS Gooch, MC and his crew who were (l to r) L/Sgt C. Haigh of Huddersfield, L/Cpl Timbrell, MM of Melksham, Wiltshire and Sgt. Barlow of Stalybridge, Cheshire. IWM BU 3128

Typhoon Rockets fitted to the turret of this M4A4 Coldstream Guards' Sherman snapped on 1 April 1945 passing the remains of a jute spinning mill in Ahaus, Germany. IWM BU 3136

Discarded pots of white paint have been used to mark out the edges of the Bailey bridge and the stone ramp onto it as tanks and infantry cross the Dortmund-Ems Canal. The infantryman of 6th Cameronians wears windproof smock and distinctive late war Turtle style helmet. The bridge had been built after a night of heavy mortar and shellfire and was a Class 40 triple single bridge, 110 ft long. This is one of the first Shermans to go over, and belongs to The Royal Scots Greys. (4 April 1945) IWM BU 3141

A IC Hybrid burns at the roadside as a Bren Carrier accelerates passed the danger. Note the cast front of the hull, along with early style bogies and VVSS suspension. W/O Camo scheme has been applied to the barrel and despite additional track sections being added to the hull and turret this tank has probably been disabled from enemy action originating in the field to the right of the road. The fire has not yet ignited the fuel tanks, oil and stowed ammunition. The photo was taken on the road to Ruurlo in Northern Holland near the German border on 2 April 1945 by Sgt Ames, AFPU. IWM BU 3151

Crab flail tanks regroup in a town square in Arnhem, this time in April 1945. Note unit markings chalked onto the side of the rollers, and the ferocious fire in the building to the right. IWM BU 3514 & 3515

BU 3169 Smoke dischargers fitted on turret, tank crosses bridge, and BU3168 an M4A4, note telephone cable reel welded to turret side of these Guards Armoured Shermans advancing into Germany on 6 April 1945. IWM BU 3169 & IWM BU 3168

M4A1 with track
extenders rumbles
through Hopsten
on 8 April 1945,
with crew wearing
great coats to
protect against the
Spring chill.
IWM BU 3324

An infantry team beckon
on this 4th Armoured
Brigade tank after
clearing houses up this
small track in the village
of Voltlage. The village
was taken in house to
house action by the
Royal Scots Fusiliers, 156
Brigade, 52nd Division
assisted by armour.
IWM BU 3329

12 April 1945. German women watch the Shermans of 1st Armoured (Coldstreams) drive on in the village of Lusche. IWM BU 3577

Lost in foliage. Somewhere in Germany the expertise and experience of the crew is revealed by this heavily camouflaged Firefly. IWM BU 5255

A IC Hybrid Firefly pulled up alongside a 75mm Hybrid in the town square of Wismar on the Baltic Coast. Both tanks of the Scots Greys were part of the farthest reaches of the British advance in the north and are heavily camouflaged with wilting bracken and pine foliage. Track extenders are visible on both tanks, and the Firefly's barrel retains its W/O camo paint scheme. The road wheels are a mix of solid plain disc and pressed ribbed type. Abandoned German vehicle, generator trailer and mobile offices litter the square. IWM BU 5308

A Guards' Firefly fitted with track extenders and an additional single 60lb Typhoon Rocket mounted on the left of the turret. Rockets of this type were uniquely fitted to tanks of the Coldstream Guards, usually in pairs or fours, just before the Rhine Crossing. They were reported to have dealt a devastating effect on German morale. This is either a Hybrid or IC as the camouflage is obscuring the front hull shape as intended. Photographed on 12 April 1945, these vehicles were from the Coldstream Guards and were firing on the woods in Lusche on the outskirts of Bremen. A Firefly spitting out 17-pounder rounds and 60lb rockets must have delivered a definitive message! IWM BU 3584

Victory parade of 51st Highland Division in Bremerhaven, 12 May 1945. Here Lieutenant General B G Horrocks, GB, DSO, MC XXX Corps Commander took the salute during a parade which included the Massed Pipes and Drums of the Division. (Note co-drivers sat cross legged for drive past.) IWM BU 6113

More Shermans participate in the Bremerhaven Victory roll past, note crew member stood to attention on rear engine decking. Hybrid IC on the left and M4A2 with paint stripped and muzzle steel polished on the right. IWM BU 6114

Sherman crossing the Kaiser Wilhelm Canal near Steenfeld on 9 May 1945. It is a 1C Hybrid model belonging to 7th Armoured Division. The turret has been reversed for travelling, and barrel locked in its gun crutch. This does reveal typical front glacis plate stowage, and the sharp nosed one piece transmission cover of the 1C Hybrid. Driver sits in raised seat position to seat out and loader and commander enjoy the sunshine. Remains of the factory fitted sand shields along one side of the tank are visible. Closer inspection again reveals the armoured plug welded into the hull MG position. IWM BU 6131

Chrysler Multibank engine is lifted from the hull of an M4A4. Note fire extinguishers mounted on rear plate and bracket mounts for the long stowage box revealed.
WM BU 6508

M4A4 centre and other models of Shermans in a base repair shop awaiting work. M5 High Speed Tractor in British livery is also used in the yard IWM BU 6519

An excellent example of the War Office Counter-Shading camo scheme for the end of the barrel of the 17-pounder mounted in the Firefly. Monty casually strolls by these weapons for Victory at an exhibition held in Paris during May 1945. The tanks have received a shiny new gloss coating and the counter-shaded camo scheme has once again been applied to demonstrate to a curious public how the longer barrel was disguised from enemy identification. IWM BU 6780

M4A6 and M4A4 models among others await maintenance work in this giant repair facility in Germany. The far wall is sign-written warning *Smoking Forbidden!* IWM BU 6946

Chapter Eight

The Far East – British Shermans up the Jungle

The photos in this chapter show armour of the British 14th Army in Burma after the jungle breakout in the last years of the war. Fighting spilled out onto the plains and created the need for the whole force to be retrained at British-run battle schools in India after years fighting in the confines of jungle. They reached the open ground after a long fight to regain the territory they had lost in the earlier retreat from the Japanese in Spring of 1942. The primary objective after Stillwell's Chinese Force and Alexander's troops had been so forcefully routed was to stop a Japanese invasion of India. Combat in the Far East had been raging since the war's declaration.

The Shermans used in Burma were few in the mid-war period but grew toward the last year of combat. Often arriving directly from America they came equipped in American standard interiors and only minor interior modification took place. Photos In this chapter even demonstrate British crews wearing American style fibre tank helmets possibly due to the better crew intercom connection achieved through them or due to the intense heat. Externally the tanks were fitted with a myriad of framework designs to dissuade Japanese magnetic mines, and to provide additional stowage potential on the hull of the tank for crew personal kit or to fasten camouflage scrim upon.

First action in the Far East however, occurred in the Pacific with the US Marine Corps at Tarawa Island in November of 1943, although I have been unable to illustrate this occurrence in the current publication. Photography from the Pacific campaign is of course abundant and demonstrates the Sherman being used in infantry support and as a mobile artillery platform as it was in parts of Italy and in Germany toward the end of the war in Europe. From the end of 1943 the Sherman was present throughout the USMC's Island Hopping campaign although rarely fought tank against tank due to inadequate and diminished operational capability of the Japanese armoured forces. No US Armoured divisions were deployed to the Pacific but specialized Sherman equipped Tank Battalions were created to support the infantry. The enemy in the Philippines posed little threat with armoured opposition however anti-tank weapons and fearless magnetic mine carrying Japanese soldiers posed a major threat. Photographs from the island-hopping operations show a range of improvised protection created by crews including basic planks of wood attached to any flat surface of the tank, to more vigorously protected versions with hundreds of nails banged through the wood in an effort to detract borders!

Returning to the Burma campaign the background to these photographs was the story of a long and arduous struggle over difficult terrain and coping with extremes of the climatic scales ranging from monsoon to drought. By mid-war and well into Sherman full production a new assault was planned to capitalize on success. The coastal Arakan district of Burma was pinpointed for assault, at the same time Wingate's experimental Chindit Operations were also authorised. At the Quebec Conference of 1943 plans were approved envisaging a counter-offensive against Japan which might have overburdened the C-In-C in India and SEAC (South East Asia Command) was established with Admiral Lord Louis Mountbatten in Supreme Command. His HQ was relocated to Kandy in Ceylon during April of 1944. His, and SEAC's main objectives was the reconquest of Burma and the opening of land communication lines with China. It was decided land operations might be undertaken in support of Stillwell's project, which were intended to open the road between Ledo and that part of Burma remaining in Chinese hands. Stillwell had to oversee the construction of the road using with Chinese troops, trained and equipped in India after the withdrawal from Burma. They were also assisted by US specialised troops and native levies. The 3rd Indian Division was also retrained as an airborne force under Wingate's direction and was planned to land on or near the Mandalay Railway.

In order to maintain pressure on the Japanese, operations in Arakan were to be resumed, Manipur based troops were to improve communications to the Chindwin Valley and also operate across the river. Both these operations were to be carried out by 14th Army men under General WJ Slim, composed of the 15th Corps in Arakan, the 3rd Corps in Manipur and the 33rd Corps held back in reserve. The dry season opened in January of 1944 and defeat of the Japanese in the Arakan soon followed. By March, the Manipur front took the focus, recce patrols probed the Chindwin valley discovering that the enemy were advancing in great strength. The 4th Corps required urgent offensive power to contain the Japanese so the 5th Division was flown immediately to the area. The danger to the railway at Dimapur matured when the Japanese sent a lightly armoured column through very rough country to strike at the main road beyond the reach of the Imphal Force. They found themselves blocked by a strong force. By the end of April 1944 the garrison at

Kohima had been relieved but the Japanese stubbornly clung on. Only after major fighting took place was contact re-established with Imphal in the middle of June. The Monsoon was by then in full blast again- howling winds, deluge of rainfall but General Slim wanted the offensive pressed home. It was the enemy that wilted under the climatic conditions. Three Japanese Divisions thrust forward toward Dimapur, but without adequate supply and communications lines and were defeated.

October brought the new dry season and Slim's offensive really gained momentum, expelling the enemy without mercy from strongpoints at Tiddim, Kennedy Peak and Fort White. Two months later bridgeheads were established across the Chindwin River. The 14th Army were ready to link with the Northern Force in an advance jointly on Mandalay. In the north General Stillwell had extended the Ledo Road 50 miles across the frontier covered by Chinese troops.

Opposition was again encountered this time from the Japanese 18th Division in the Mukaung Valley but support arrived in the form of Wingate's 3rd Division which was landed in the Katha Region although it was during this time that Wingate himself was killed in an air-crash. A two pronged assault under Stillwell's guidance pressed ahead, the main force fighting at Kamaing just short of Mogaung. A Chindit column comprising South Staffordshires, Lancashire Fusiliers and Gurkhas captured Kamaing on 26 June. Stillwell had now gained a firm footing in the dry region of Northern Burma by early July. At Mogaung he had captured the main Japanese northern supply depot, without supplies in the jungle defeat was only a matter of time. He had also captured valuable airfields for Allied re-supply use. His main body, bolstered by the 36th Division began to advance along the Mandalay Railway, while his Chinese troops were sent to take Bhamo. Bhamo was the head of navigation on the Irrawaddy River, this was also significantly the start point of the road which linked Burma to China. In December a foothold in Bhamo had been won and another Chinese column had crossed the Irrawaddy between Bhamo and Katha. By 10 December Katha fell. Ahead, lay the open country in which tanks could operate freely and air strips were plentiful. The fate of the Imperial Japanese Army was sealed.

The M4A4 tank, carrying its own camouflage bundle and Infantry team move forward on the battlefield in the far east IWM SE 1227

Camouflaged and firing a group of Shermans send over shells. IWM SEU 1228

The Myebon Landing of January, 1945. This photograph was taken by Sgt Titmus as Shermans move forward on open plains acting on demand from the infantry who met strong opposition IWM SE 2188

11 January 1945. 3 Commando and M4 or M4A4 armoured support embark toward the Myebon Peninsular from Akyab Island. The original caption described these Sherman tanks as dealing 'ponderous blows to the already demoralised Japanese.' IWM SE 2301

62 Motorised Bde advance on a road between Myaungyu on the Irrawaddy Bridgehead and Meiktila. IWM SE 3071

The Probyn's Horse of the 14th Army attack Kaing on the route to Meiktila. The Probyn's Horse had a long military tradition originated during the Indian Mutiny when Sir John Lawrence, the Chief Commissioner of the Punjab ordered two regiments of Sikh irregular cavalry to be raised. In 1860 Major Dighton Probyn VC became commanding officer of one of these regiments, uniformed and trained these experienced horsemen and the regiment became known as Probyn's Horse thereafter. IWM SE 3073

Photographed by Sgt R Stubbs (AFPU), Infantry and Shermans of the 17th Division move roll on toward Meiktila in a revenge powered lightning advance in memory of their stand on the Imphal-Kohima Road in 1944, and their fighting withdrawal from Burma earlier in the war. Here men of the 6/7 Rajput Rifles use the Sherman hull as cover. Smoke from a burning village obscures the field. 23 February 1945 IWM SE 3094 & IWM SE 3095

Men from 6/7 Rajput Rifles return from a search of wooded country around Meiktila and climb aboard Shermans of The Probyn's Horse. A good view is provided of the BC-1362 Interphone Box for tank-infantry communication. IWM SE 3099

Sherman at the Irrawaddy Bridgehead river crossing. Elsewhere men of the Norfolk Regiment and 18th Field Regiment, RA in Priests were laying down a barrage to cover. IWM SE 3167

Fighting in Mandalay narrows to one strongly held Japanese fortress at the civic and governmental centre of the city and the full force of the allied 19th Division. Troops move through the suburbs of the town and the mopping up begins in the ruins. Here Grant tanks, in far more frequent numbers in Burma than the Sherman and infantry close inwards to where the enemy stills holds out. IWM SE 3297

Sherman crossing on a company issue 'Scissors Bridge' which could be carried on a tank and utilised local boats to cross small rivers. Here it easily takes the weight of a tank. IWM SE 3424

Fighting on southwards the tank crews that came from the Middle East to continue the fight in the Far East. Battle taxi – ferried up to the front on the engine deck of a Sherman. IWM SE 3486

'Cairngorm' – Sherman of the Gordon Highlanders

Cpl Wilson lubricating track wheels with a grease gun to keep Cairngorm, his tank, in fighting condition. This series of photographs from 15 March 1945 taken by Sgt Stubbs (AFPU) details the daily grind of an all-Scots tank crew. The series features Captain J M Weir, of Glasgow the Tank and Squadron Commander, Sgt B Smith of Lanarkshire who was Co-driver and Troop Sergeant, Cpl L Wilson of Roxburgh who was driver, Cpl J Picken of Aberdeen who was Radio Operator and Tpr A Morrison of Aberdeenshire who was Gunner. The set of photographs was taken when Cairngorm formed part of the armoured advance from Taungtha to Meiktila which was captured on 3 March. They belong to 116 Royal Armoured Corps Regiment (Gordon Highlanders.) IWM SE 3506

Bombing up – Sgt Smith hands a 75mm round to Cpl Wilson. Trooper Morrison is in the turret as Cpl Picken handles machine gun ammunition for the bow mounted weapon. IWM SE 3507

Cpl Picken and Tpr Morrison (left) cleaning the barrel rifling of grease, dirt, dust and debris. IWM SE 3509

The Squadron Commander now briefs his crew, (l to r) Wilson, Picken, Morrison, and Weir. Also Sgt Smith and Captain B T Smith of the Orkney Islands listen in. Note spare track pins neatly stored IWM SE 3511

On the Taungtha Road a Sherman is photographed against typical Burmese back drop of Pagoda IWM SE 3513.

Wearing US tank crew helmets Sgt Smith and Cpl Wilson (right) throw open the hatches for fresh air after a fierce engagement with the Japanese. Captain Picken surveys the aftermath of battle from the turret. IWM SE 3515

Tpr Morrison emerges from the turret to suck in some deep breathes of air after the tank had been involved in a four hour battle in the area around the Pagoda. The Japanese were dug in using concealed positions everywhere but were forced to retreat after a fierce exchange of Cairngorm's 75mm ammunition. Note Commander's turret ring detail, casting marks, part numbers. IWM SE 3516

There is never an end to the fighting day, but the crew of Cairngorm find some time to stop for dinner after the battle and attempt to relax for the evening before being called into action again. IWM SE 3518

Repairing Battle-Damaged Shermans in Burma

Keeping Shermans in action around Taungtha are men of the Royal Electrical Mechanichal Engineers and I.E.M.E (Indian.) Here they are photographed in March 1945 at 5th Indian Division Tank Workshops. Final adjustments are made to a multibank engine, after its donor tank took a direct hit from a 105mm shell. This engine has been completely rebuilt and is positioned for refitting into a new vehicle. IWM SE 3617

Electrical welding of appliqué armour plates over driver and co-driver's positions on another vehicle which has suffered battle damage but which can be returned to action after this work order has been carried out. Note the rough edges of field applied additional armour plate.
IWM SE 3618

Removing the 75mm gun from a Sherman at the workshops of 5th Indian Division Workshops at Taungtha. Work will be completed at maximum speed and effort to return the tank to action just as soon as it is ready. IWM SE 3621

New T62 track sections being adjusted, note defining three rivet heads on each track block, and the curved nature of the steel track cuff. This is L/Cpl Watson, 116 RAC Regiment (Gordon Highlanders) at work in the 5th Indian Division Workshop. IWM SE 3626

An elephant liberated from the Japanese who had themselves captured it and put it to work, races a Sherman in friendly rivalry. Two giants of the battlefield with much the same concept behind both. The native crew on top of the elephant shouted across that their weapon was cheaper to run and much more lovable! The Sherman Crew shouted back that they weren't arguing, but they felt a lot safer inside their tank! The elephant went on to devour the crew's supply of army biscuits shortly after the photograph was posed. (March, 1945) IWM SE 3640

The crew themselves often had to repair track damage and breakage. Here they prepare new T54E1 Track, denoted by angular edges to the fabricated steel cuffs on each track block, for fitting to another Sherman of 116 R.A.C Regiment, Gordon Highlanders in the Meiktila area. (l to r) Sgt. Crawley of Lanarkshire, Cpl Adams of Aberdeen, Tpr Craik of Berwick-On-Tweed and Tpr Milne of Aberdeen. IWM SE 3697

Operation DRACULA, the amphibious attack begun on the muddy plains of a river beach head south of Rangoon. 14th Army were coming from the south around Meiktila and were intent on meeting up with their colleagues moving up from the south. Armor pushing ahead in these shots. IWM SE 3936

Infantry and Shermans move forward watched by a Bren team. No. 2 has a spare barrel tied over his back on the right, as the field is sprayed with Japanese sniper fire. IWM SE 3942

1 May 1945 and the war in the Far East is slowly coming to its close. Pegu, a vital road and rail junction some fifty miles north of Rangoon, was liberated in May, 14th Army troops engulfed the area in their sweep southward to the coast. Here Sherman tanks roll on past the blazing outskirts of Pegu
IWM SE 3956

Chapter Nine

US Shermans – Wartime American Action

The M4 Sherman first experienced combat with American forces in Tunisia shortly after it went into action with the British. A platoon of 2nd Armoured Division which was attached to 2nd Battalion, 13th Armoured regiment of five tanks which were all knocked out clashed with the enemy south-west of Tebourba on 6 December – a disastrous beginning to the long combat career of the tank with US Forces. All five losses did occur against well concealed anti-tank guns and professionally deployed enemy tanks. The harsh early lessons were learnt and absorbed quickly. A week later and 26 M4A1's supported the British 1st Guards Brigade in the fierce fighting on Longstop Hill and with these two actions the American crews had been blooded and initiated with combat inside the Sherman Tank.

At the close of action in North Africa the M4 and M4A1 had become the standard tanks for US Armoured forces, supplemented by a number of M4A3's which arrived in Italy after the fall of Rome on 5 June 1944. Other models followed and as reports of the first engagements filtered back to the United States a race was begun to test and incorporate improvements in newer models of the successful tank. Every area of the Sherman was considered including attempting to increase mobility, finding big more powerful armament, more explosive ammunition and better protection for the crew and stowed ammunition. A variety of new track blocks and suspension systems were also tried out. Shermans were able to incorporate many of these changes on the production line and improved versions began rolling out of the factories in preparation for the invasion of Europe. Tanks equipped with larger 76mm guns and 105mm howitzers were sent straight to Britain. The crews awaiting their new equipment were not all impressed by the improvements. While the 105mm was instantly accepted the 76mm versions caused some consternation which is easy to understand when one considers the crews had all trained with 75mm versions throughout their time in armour and confidence in the new 76 was going to be difficult to achieve in the short period of time before the invasion was to commence. All of the units that landed on D-Day in fact went ashore with 75mm versions but it is interesting to note that by the end of the European campaign over half of all Shermans serving with US units were then equipped with the 76mm main gun.

Once the landings had taken place US armoured columns spread westward to Brittany and then swung south-east into the French heartland supported from the air by P47 Thunderbolts in a similar role to the Typhoons above the British advance. Tank-infantry teams worked in harmony village by village and the terrain was one that suited the Sherman exactly. Its speed and reliability helped it motor on rapidly through the lanes and fields into the German rear areas. Just the type of speedy motorized advance America favoured, to the point the crews began collecting anything that would help them cross obstacles in their path. Later photos in this chapter demonstrate the collection of telegraph pole straight pine trunks, affixed to the side of many Shermans entering Germany. These were not only there to provide protection against rocket attack, but as the photographs demonstrate, facilitated the easy traversing of rail track without damaging the rails of the tank tracks. Other forms of protection for the hull show frameworks of chicken wire holding in a hundred sand bags as an additional outer layer deterrent to the *Panzerfaust*.

The Sherman tank in American service was deployed all over the world but the heaviest concentration was in Europe hence I have only chosen examples from the European campaign in this chapter. By the war's end, every variant and every production type was in service with the US Army's fifteen divisions and thirty-seven tank battalions. Here are a few of them captured on film.

Ike and Air Chief Marshal Tedder watching M4A1 tank firing at Warminster Barracks miniature range. During their tour they visited the US XIX Corps, 3rd Armoured Division and heard a pipe band of 51st Highland Division. In H36304 Monty and Ike watch US 33rd Armoured Division troops demonstrate the 75mm Sherman Gun's accuracy on the West Down Range, Warminster. IWM H 36298. IWM H 36304 features 'Hopalong' fitted with additional cheek armour applied to the turret and hull sides.

Fresh replacement M4A1 being craned ashore in the South of France which will be made ready for the advance. IWM OWIL 677659

Infantry and M4 tank team in Angers, Brittany. No details of date are provided. The Infantry have tucked field jackets into webbing, wear HBT trousers so was probably taken in mid summer 1944. The original caption is marked 'SHAEF Approved'. IWM EA 33049

Shermans leave track indentations across the battlefield as troops in foxholes watch. One is struck by what an easy method this must have been to pinpoint armoured movement from the air.
IWM EA 45772

Sinking in the mud, urgent efforts being made to free this Sherman 'Mr Gooch', either an M4 or M4A4 variant of 7th Armoured. Note US M1936 Musette bags hung over the blade sight, headlamps fitted and appliqué armour shields welded in front of driver's hoods. IWM IA 40837

Blacked out stars on this travelling M4 as infantry pass in opposite direction. IWM OWIL 32078

Tank infantry co-operation in very close proximity. A sharp nosed M4A3 operates under the direction of a house clearing squad inside a French village. IWM KY 28044

Infantry ride up to the front on an M4A1 (76) (W) Sherman. Infantry carry extra clips of 30.06 ammunition in cotton bandoliers slung across their shirts and jackets. IWM EA 33431

An M4 Sherman of 7th US Army in French town razed to the ground by retreating Germans and aerial bombardment. IWM EA 45001

M4A3 Shermans , with turret and all hatch apertures sealed with bitumen ready for transportation from Calais to the Pacific Theatre are checked by Quartermaster staff. IWM FRA 204514

Infantry crouch in cover across the street as a heavily camouflaged Sherman engages a target between houses. The commander utilises the .50 HMG as well. IWM EA 36533

The photographer's shadow caught on the recently ploughed field as the M4A1 Sherman in the foreground begins to heat up seconds after taking a direct hit. Other heavily camouflaged M4 Shermans trundle past in the background. IWM EA 38142

Emerging from a hedgerow onto a country lane one crewman makes certain a downed telegraph pole and line don't infringe upon the late model M4 with combination rolled and cast hull (note rounded front end) as other infantrymen keep watch on the road. IWM EA 29531

Blacked out stars also feature on these US M4 Shermans as do orange allied aerial recognition sheets spread across the engine decking. IWM HU 82154

Recovery onto an M25 Rogers Heavy Trailer. Note double wading funnels which facilitated inlet and exhaust access in heavy surf. IWM EA 14674

Collected armoured right-offs from the battlefield ready for rebuild and repair. Fire damage is apparent on both the Shermans nearest camera.
IWM EA 200157

Wreck recovery and rebuilding Shermans – salvaged live ammunition is piled on the floor. M10 tank destroyers receive the same treatment as the M4A2 and A3 variants in the foreground. Note impact points and destroyed field boots hanging near the headlight guards. IWM EA 44273

New crated radial engines arrive from the US. IWM EA 33146

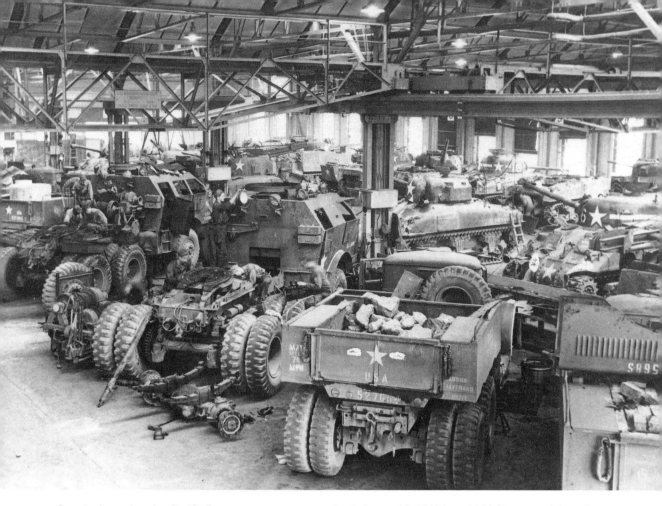

Repair depot interior. Pacific Dragon wagons are serviced along with M4A1 and M4 Shermans. Note the solid white stripe painted around the turrets. IWM NYF 37225

Repairing a direct hit. Here an armoured plug is welded into the hole and only a small amount of damage along the edge of where the sandshields attach remains visible. The Sherman M4A4 exhibited at Lambeth's Imperial War Museum contains just such a repair to it's turret. IWM EA 43240

M4 – Fording a French river, note the abundance of Allied ID stars covering the rear of the tank. IWM EA 37649

HM The King inspects US Armoured troops and M4/M4A3 tanks from the comfort of a Dodge Command car at the close of the North African campaign. The King was escorted by Lieutenant Eddy, General Omar N Bradley, General Mark Clark, Lieutenant General George S Patton and Major General Geoffrey Keyes. IWM NA 3610

Actual battlefield patrol photography is very rare. Here US Infantry partnered with Sherman M4A1 (W) 76 advance across some open ground to the rise of the next hill in the Bocage. Cameraman peers through a hedgerow to snap away then follows in the muddy tracks of the troop laden tanks. IWM EA 30973

Staff Sergeant Cullin and his Hedgerow Device

Actual photo of Staff Sergeant Cullin of the 102nd Cavalry Recconaissance Squadron & Cullin's invention being produced as the beach obstacles from Omaha Beach are cut by Engineers and remanufactured into the anti-hedgerow teeth welded to the transmission covers of so many tanks in Normandy. They have become known as THE CULLIN HEDGEROW DEVICE. Often thought to be an American adaptation only, there are plenty of photographs in the Normandy section of this book showing them fitted to British tanks too. Driven at speed toward the thick growing Bocage hedgerows a Sherman fitted with a Cullin hedgerow device could literally uproot the centuries old growth and cut a neat Sherman-wide channel through the foliage into the next field. Tactics employed a three tank manoeuvre where the cutter tank ripped open the hole, and following tanks would break left and right covering all angles for advance. Field by field they could then push through the Bocage. Cullin won the Legion of Merit award for his innovative device. IWM EA36302 & IWM PL 32441

M4A1 Sherman with field modified appliqué armour plating on the hull sides. Field modified appliqué fittings had much rougher edges than that fitted by the factories. It is towed by a Lee ARV IWM PL 26066

Infantry advance in support of the Shermans which exhibit blacked out stars, note the remains of Allied Star on the turret of tank nearest the camera. This is a 47 degree sloped hull front M4A3.
IWM EA 38102

Passing battered anti-tank weapons and abandoned jeeps this Sherman accelerates at speed up the road toward the smoke and fighting. IWM EA 34014

Sharp nosed late production M4A2 Sherman fitted with M3 75mm main gun. Glacis plate is loaded with loose track extenders as it motors down a cobbled street and the siren is centrally located rather than on front wing. Note the T48 rubber track blocks fitted have flattened out with wear, whereas the track spares mounted on the Sherman hull have new recently moulded cuff definition. Odd track extenders are fitted here and there on the tracks. Perhaps this tank was ordered to move on mid fitting, and the job is to be completed at a later stage. M34A1 gun mount and rotor shield are fitted to carry the 75mm gun. Appliqué armour has been added to the left cheek of the turret and to protect the ammo stored within the tank hull. Crew wear M1 infantry steel helmets. Note additional attachments welded to front diff cover towing eyes. IWM EA 58373

Late production M4A3 (76) W HVSS provides a view of the distinctive 76mm main gun muzzle brake and barrel length. Here it uses logs to cross a railway track without damaging the valuable rails. Logs were not only attached to the side of the hull for increased armour protection. This tank exhibits the redesigned turret, and also mounts both a .50 AA HMG by the loaders hatch but a .30 MG for the commander to use. The horizontal volute spring suspension (HVSS) is also illustrated well.
IWM EA 63462

US M32B2 Recovery Shermans – American ARV

An M32B2 Recovery Vehicle based on the Sherman chassis of 4th Armoured Division in the Nancy sector on 11 November 1944. Note the 81mm Mortar for which thirty rounds of smoke ammunition were carried. This was to be deployed as the giant 60,000 pound Garwood winch seen stowed along the hull was utilised to recover knocked out and disabled armour. The crew entertain local children in the freezing slush by cooking over an impromptu BBQ built up on the mounting for the front towing eye.
IWM EA 43979

M32B2 Recovery Shermans, amongst others unloaded on the French coast at Cherbourg are serviced by ordnance crews in Spring 1945 as part of priority order to help strengthen the final advance into the Reich. The tanks were then put on rail cars and shipped up to the front. IWM EA 44263

Spotted in convoy through the Austrian Alps the centre tank is an M4A3 (76) W HVSS. Note the loaders head protruding through additional turret hatch, larger tracks and turret and barrel length confirming the larger 76mm gun fitted with muzzle brake. IWM AP 66220

M4A1 heavily camouflaged crossing Pont Aristide Briand bridge where US Army Engineers have already thrown a span across the breaks dynamited into the bridge by the Germans as they retreated from Laval. IWM FRA 100189

Unusually camouflaged M4A3's roll between Bocage hedgerows, with this American camouflage more reminiscent of British schemes. IWM EA 30986

Unusual snow camouflage on this distant M4A3 (76) W. Often white wash or even local fence paint was acquired after a heavy snow fall by the crew! Even at this distance the turret shape and barrel length are easily identifiable. IWM EA 51287

Rolling through the cobbled streets of Mannheim, a similar M4A3 (76) W HVSS Sherman exhibits the M4A3 unique exhaust vents in this poor quality shot. A British pattern jerry can is mounted on the front hull step along with individual sections of spare track. Large amounts of kit are still being stowed on the rear engine deck to maximise room in the fighting compartment of the tank. The crew wear the infantry style M1 steel helmet and not the specifically styled fibre tank crewman's helmet. IWM KY 60968

Stuart Light Tank with Howitzer and Sherman M4A1 (76)W HVSS alike all contribute to this line up of mobile artillery somewhere in Germany.
IWM EA 32827

Alternative camouflage in the form of heavily wrapped strapping secures kit to the hull but also acts to totally break the outline shape of the tank up. The censor has obliterated Unit identification markings on the diff cover but large driver's and co-driver's hatch lids, sharp nosed diff cover plus commander's cuppola indicate this is an M4A1 (76) W Sherman. A .50 HMG is mounted on the loader's hatch ring on top the turret. An M8 Staghound armoured recce car is parked at the side of the road as civilians gather to watch the advance. A mix of infantry steel and tanker's fibre crew helmets are worn. IWM KY 55590

Devastation in Germany as a M4A3 (76) W HVSS Sherman slowly claws it's way across the rubble guided by an infantry scout who has climbed onto the engine deck to converse with the tank commander. Armour such as this faced increasing threat from the handheld *Panzer Faust* and *Schrek* as weaponry of an increasingly desperate enemy. Pre-war reserves of *Whermacht* armour had long been expended. One can imagine the clear target armour presented from the shadows of destroyed housing! IWM EA 61747

Directed by an MP and kicking up dust down a French road this Sherman M4 wears bright orange aerial recognition panel across the engine deck to warn off allied fighter bombers from friendly fire. An experience military planners are still wrestling to combat in 2005. IWM EA 30917

Stunned civilians look on as a Sherman M4A3 rolls into the centre of a German town. The war has clearly only weeks left to run its course although the tank still wears it's name 'DESTINATION?' proudly. IWM S&G 72847A

Snow begins to lay on this abandoned Sherman during the Ardennes offensive. No visible damage leads to the conclusion that mechanical failure had stopped the vehicle. It is either an M4 or M4A4.
IWM EA 44023

The icy conditions prove too much for this Sherman based M10 Tank Destroyer which has slid sideways down the bank and turned over spilling the contents of the open topped turret. This predicament does provide a good view of the front crew escape hatch in the floor which could be knocked through with hammer or heavy wrench to provide an escape route for the crew in emergency under the vehicle. IWM EA 49114

Passing a knocked out German anti-tank gun the frontal protection piled upon this Sherman clearly demonstrates the fear of attack by *Panzerfaust* or *Panzer Shrek* Rocket in the closing stages of the Second World War. With diminishing supplies of both A/T ammunition and guns, Volksturm and remnants of the Army resorted to the hand held throwaway rocket launchers in large numbers. IWM EA 59330

Infantry ride the decks of these Shermans moving in column through a devastated village. It was the infantry tank partnership eventually adopted by the Allies that helped stem the horrific tank losses in the Italian and early Normandy campaigns. Mutual protection and heavier firepower than small arms when required. IWM EA 60052

Chapter Ten

Model List – Identifying Sherman Variants

The first thing to stress when discussing the identification of Sherman Models is that with only a cursory glance it is a very difficult task. With further examination, and detail comparison it becomes a very difficult, time consuming and frustrating task! Essentially they do all look the same to the novice, and it is often in the small detail such as type of periscopes fitted, locations of hatches or shapes of castings that the identification process can begin to be addressed. Relying on the shape of the transmission cover at the front of tank alone however is not sufficient. That method has often been given as the sure-fire method to identify a Sherman variant. The transmission covers appear to have been interchangeable with all models, and therefore with workshop and repair facilities at the front line and in rear areas working overtime to replace damaged vehicles this feature alone cannot be a definitive identification trick to use. Look at the chaotic repair depot scenes in the American chapter and you see live ammunition rolling around the workshop floor next to welding equipment and oil coated engine filters. Were they really going to take the time to request a three part cover when a pile of spare solid one piece cast covers lay outside? Plus there were many 'in service' adaptations which were carried out by each individual crew, or Unit modifications to the basic tank configuration. Views of the rear armour plate provide further assistance. The M4 rear plate is more vertical, and shallower often with a cut-out that reveals two of the engine's air cleaners and small exhaust pipes compared with the deeper deck which overhangs the rear plate of the M4A4 type. The M4A2 and M4A3 also have the deeper rear plates but the M4A2's exhaust system is unique to its type and looks nothing like the M4A3 or M4A4 variants' exhausts. These have huge exhaust pipes with a single rear engine access hatch door. Later model M4A2's and M4A3's were fitted with exhaust deflector units. The stowage areas for tools on the rear decking and rear engine access door layout also provides indications of the type of engine and variant one is looking at. Only by studying many different photographs will the reader begin to seek out the differentiating features that mark out each model. In brief - look at rear decking, type of hull construction, exhaust layout, transmission covers, turret and gun type, suspension units, and engine access doors among the main distinguishing features.

THE BASIC TURRET TANK MODELS

The tables in this chapter give an idea of Sherman turret tank production and acceptances during Second World War, however to appreciate the extent of the Sherman family of AFV's one must consider the range of adaptations that were built on the Sherman M4 chassis too. Not illustrated in the pages of this book in depth are Tank Destroyers like the M10, Achilles and M36 Jackson nor are Self-Propelled Gun Howitzers like the Priest and Sexton featured. There were other variants such as Canal Defence, Troop Carriers, Flame Throwers, Rocket Launchers, Prime Movers, Experimental and Test vehicles.

Unfortunately the parametres set for this book have limited the photographic scope. Thus only some examples of BARV, ARV and other funnies have been illustrated. To help further identify models within the family of Sherman vehicles here are some distinguishing features on model variants in the basic turret tank models. Letter designations denote the following:

'T' – Experimental Type, 'E' – Experimental Modification, 'M' – Standardised Type, 'A' – Standardised Modification and 'B' – Standardised Chassis Variation.

Here is a basic guide:

MODEL M4

Featured welded hull, cast turret, and 75mm gun in an M34 gun mount. Vision slots were fitted into front hull. Differential (transmission) housing was three part, bolted together. The earliest examples, after standardization in October 1941 had the track return rollers mounted at the top centre on the bogies. Engine mounted was the Continental R975 9 Cylinder Radial. Production continued until January, 1944 and later models had the 75mm gun mounted in the M34A1 gun mount. The later M4's also had the three piece differential cover replaced by the sharp nosed design manufactured as a one piece casting. Therefore later M4's are often misidentified as M4A2 variants. Sand shields were factory fitted on the M4.

MODEL M4A1

Two months after the standardization of the M4 in 1941 came the M4A1 which featured a curved cast hull to lessen the impact of direct hits after testing raised concern. The first Sherman accepted into British Service 'Michael' was an example of this model and is illustrated in this book. It used the three piece bolted differential cover and also direct vision slots in the front of the hull. These did not rotate, hence 'direct' vision slot - front view only. The 75mm gun was again mounted in the M34 mount. Track return rollers were centred atop the bogies on early models and there were ports cut in the front of the hull to allow the bow mounting of two fixed .30 calibre machine guns. These were later sealed and deleted by end of 1941. The engine used was the Continental R975 Radial engine. Later production models rolled off the line with track return rollers moved to the rear of the bogies, a cast one piece rounded diff cover and appliqué armour neatly welded to the turret and hull sides for added protection of ammunition compartments within. Field applied additional armour plate usually has a much rougher welded seam where it had been applied to the hull. Some were factory fitted with gun travelling locks attached at the front of the hull.

MODEL M4A2

Also standardized in December of 1941 this model had a welded hull with a cast turret and looked similar to an M4. Power to propel the tank was provided by the twin General Motors 6-71 Diesel engines. Earliest production tanks had the 75mm M3 in an M34 mount with vision slots for driver and co-driver. Differential cover was of the three piece bolted type and it still retained the twin fixed .30 machine guns mounted in the bow. The track return rollers were centred atop the bogies. Later versions of the M4A2 used the return rollers mounted at the rear of the bogies. Complicating identification, some early models used the one piece differential cover too, and later models of the M4A2 used this cover exclusively. 75mm guns were later mounted in the M34A1 redesigned mount and appliqué armour was added. Plates were welded onto the hull as hatch guards, especially in front of the driver's position on what has become known as the driver's hood. Gun travelling locks were fitted, and sand shields, at the factory although did not last long in the field. Battlefield travel soon tore off various components of the bolt together sand shield, which was made of much thinner steel than the armoured hull. The very late model of the M4A2 used the 47 degree hull front armour plate, which produced a distinctive silhouette rising to the driver's/ co-driver's positions. Enlarged doors for the driver and co driver were added in this later production. The diff cover used on these very late production models was of the sharp nose type only. The best way to identify this variant is by looking at the rear deck layout as the diesel engined M4A2's had a distinctive access hatch layout, of course not every photograph affords this opportunity!

MODEL M4A3

This model became standardised in January of 1942, featuring a welded hull and cast turret. The 500hp Ford tank engine was the power-plant used to motivate the M4A3. A huge eight cylinder, liquid cooled V-Type engine specifically designed for tank use. The M34 gun mount was used in early production, vision slots were fitted and the diff cover was of the cast one piece rounded nose type. Return rollers were mounted on the rear of the rollers. Later production models of the M4A3 had periscopes fitted instead of direct vision slots, and had sand shields. The M34 gun mount remained in the turret. Changes occurred with the very late production

M4A3 which mounted the 75mm gun in the M34A1 gun mount, used a vision cupola for the commander and innovated the small oval hatch above the loader in the turret. 47 degree hull front armour plate was also used on the very late production models, with enlarged driver's doors, and the cast one piece sharp nosed differential housing. Vertical Volute Spring Suspension system and sand-shields were fitted at the factory. The front armour plate also had a gun travelling lock bolted to it.

MODEL M4A4

Standardised in February 1942, and similar again to the M4 it was powered by the unique Chrysler 5 block Chrysler Multibank engine. The hull had to be lengthened to accommodate this new engine and this was noted as the first large-scale significant change to the basic Sherman design. It was elongated by 11 inches, (28cm). Consequently the bogies were spaced further apart than on other models. A longer track with 83 shoes, compared to 79 on other M4 variants was necessary. This spacing can be measured in photographs as being approximately three track end connectors long, whereas other models are only two connectors length apart. M4A4's can be identified by the tubular grille featuring on the upper rear deck directly behind the turret but these also feature on the M4A6. Earliest models mounted the 75mm M3 gun in the standard M34 mount, used vision slots in the frontal armour and were fitted with the three piece bolted differential cover. The late 1943 production model had the M34 gun mount replaced by the M34A1 and earlier vision slots were deleted. Periscopes provided front view for the drivers when hatches were battened down. The late production types still retained the three piece cover for the differential. The Chrysler designed M4A4 also features a small welded plate to either side of the turret splash ring, protecting drainage holes, which was also used on the M4A6 - These are the only types of Sherman with this feature.

MODEL M4A5

The M4A5 was produced in Canada as the Ram II tank and was only given the designation for record purposes by the US Government. The Ram II was not a Sherman variant in reality but is illustrated in the Home Army Chapter of this book, and is noted to help distinguish the other Shermans.

MODEL M4A6

This version also had the lengthened hull the same as the M4A4, but this time to accommodate an Ordnance RD-1820 air cooled diesel engine. The longer tracks with 83 shoes were also used. Interestingly the hull of the M4A6 was a composite made of rolled and cast upper hull utilising the cast one piece sharp nosed differential housing. Main gun was the 75mm in an M34A1 gun mount and suspension operated on vertical volute spring system. Sand shields were fitted in the factory as was some appliqué armour. Only a small number of M4A6's were constructed (75) between October of 1943 and February of 1944. The US Army declined their issue however some were sent to the United Kingdom. They are identifiable in British service by the large curved exhaust cover on the rear plate among other features.

MODEL M4 (105mm Howitzer)
US armament design studies had predicted the mounting of the 105mm Howitzer in a turret tank as early as 1941 and tests had been carried out in March of 1942 at the Aberdeen Proving Grounds in Maryland. The idea being to increase firepower additional to the speed of a medium tank. Prototype test models termed M4E5 & M4A4E1 had been built, tested and deemed successful. They lead to standardised versions known as the M4 (105mm Howitzer) and M4A3 (105mm Howitzer) in July 1943. Production followed a year later with the M4 105mm Howitzer mounted in an M52 gun mount with co-axial .30 calibre machine gun. 66 Howitzer rounds were carried and distinguishing features included a gun ring hatch for the commander and a small oval hatch in the turret top for loader entry. The differential housing was of the sharp nosed one piece casting, and the hull front also featured the 47 degree slope. Vertical volute springs and sand-shields were initially factory fitted but later models featured a wider track and horizontal volute suspension system.

MODEL M4A3 (105mm Howitzer)
The M4A3 105 can be distinguished by vision cupola fitting for the commander and again the oval loaders hatch on the turret top surface. Two ventilators were also fitted on the turret top. 47 degree hull front featured and the cast one piece sharp nosed differential cover completed it's frontal profile.

MODEL M4A3E2
Recognition that the second front would require an up-rated assault tank promoted development work which began in early 1944 to redesign the Sherman. To fullfil this role as an infantry support vehicle in an assault situation a new tank altogether was required, but the Pershing T26E1 had not yet passed it's testing stage or acceptance for issue within the US Army. Standard M4A3 tanks were earmarked for beefing up to take the punishment an assault tank might expect in the meantime. Additional armour was welded to front surfaces, creating a thickness in places of four inches. New turrets were designed and fitted with the 75mm M3 gun. These had six inches of frontal armour, and additional rolled plating to the top of the turret. Unfortunately the increased armour, pushing the total weight to forty-two tons meant a decrease in speed. 254 Assault tanks of the M4A3E2 type were ordered and these were produced in Michigan at the Grand Blanc Tank Arsenal from May to June, 1944.

SHERMANS DISTRIBUTED UNDER INTERNATIONAL AID PROGRAMMES

Turret Tank Type	UK	USSR	Other	International Aid Total
Medium tank, M4	2096		53	2,149
Medium tank, M4A1	942		4	946
Medium tank, M4A2	5041	1990	382	7,413
Medium tank, M4A3	7			7
Medium tank, M4A4	7167	2	274	7,443
Medium tank, M4 (105)	593			593
Medium tank, M4A1 (76) W	1330			1,330
Medium tank, M4A2 (76) W	5	2073		2,078

TURRET TANK ACCEPTANCE FIGURES FROM 1941-45 PRODUCTION
The models that passed final inspection for issue

Type	Commencing	Ended	Totals
M4	Ocotober 1941	January 1944	6748
M4A1	February 1942	December 1943	6281
M4A2	April 1942	May 1944	8053
M4A3	June 1942	September 1943	1690
M4A4	July 1942	September 1943	7499
M4A5 – US Designation or Canadian Built RAM II Tank			
M4A6	October 1943	February 1944	75
M4 (105)	February 1944	March 1945	1641
M4A1 (76) W	January 1944	July 1945	3426
M4A2 (76) W	May 1944	May 1945	2915
M4A3 (75) W	February 1944	March 1945	3071
M4A3 (76) W	March 1944	April 1945	4542
M4A3 (105)	May 1944	June 1945	3039
M4A3 E2 (Assault)	June 1944	July 1944	254

Total Sherman Production between Feb 1942 to July 1945:   **49,234**

BRITISH ARMY WARTIME DESIGNATIONS
FOR SHERMANS ACCEPTED INTO SERVICE

SHERMAN I	M4 Turret Tank with 75mm gun Mounted
SHERMAN HYBRID I	M4 Cast Glacis Plate, 75mm Gun Mounted
SHERMAN IB	M4 Turret Tank with 105mm Howitzer Mounted
SHERMAN IBY	M4, 105mm Howitzer and larger 23" track Fitted
SHERMAN IC	M4 with 17 Pdr AT Gun fitted
SHERMAN II	M4A1 with 75mm Gun
SHERMAN IIA	M4A1 with 76mm Gun
SHERMAN IIB	M4A1 with 105mm Howitzer
SHERMAN IIC	M4A1 with 17 Pdr AT gun Fitted
SHERMAN III	M4A2 with 75mm Gun
SHERMAN IIIAY	M4A2 with 76mm and 23" Tracks
SHERMAN IV	M4A3 with 75mm Gun
SHERMAN IVA	M4A3 with 76mm Gun
SHERMAN IVB	M4A3 With 105mm Howitzer
SHERMAN IVC	M4A3 with 17 Pdr
SHERMAN V	M4A4 with 75mm Gun
SHERMAN V (GUARDS)	M4A4 With turret mounted Typhoon Rocket Projectors, plus main 75mm
SHERMAN VC FIREFLY	M4A4 with 17 Pdr AT Gun
SHERMAN VII	M4A6 with 75mm Gun
SHERMAN VIIC	M4A6 with 17Pdr

US ARMY TECHNICAL MANUAL AND SUPPLY CATALOGUES

Wartime Technical Manuals (TM's) describe the technical operation of various mechanisms within the tank and also basic field maintenance procedure, but the Supply Catalogue (SNL – Standard Nomenclature List) is a huge listing of every constituent part used in the assembly of each model of tank. These were used as much more detailed reference for repair and overhaul in the workshop. Here is a reference list to help identification of original or reprinted manuals as they occasionally turn up for sale on auction websites such as Ebay, and might even turn up in your second hand bookshop!

Model	Technical Manual	Supply Catalogue
Tank, Medium, M4, 75mm Gun	TM 9-731A	SNL G-104 Vol: 6
Tank, Medium, M4 105mm Howitzer	TM 9-731AA	SNL G-104 Vol:14
Tank, Medium, M4A1, 75mm Gun	TM 9-731A	SNL G-104 Vol:11
Tank, Medium, M4A1, 76mm Gun	TM 9-731AA	SNL G-207
Tank, Medium, M4A3, 75mm Gun	TM 9-759	SNL G-204/G-104
Tank, Medium, M4A3, 75mm Gun (W)	TM 9-759 & TM 9-7018 (1954)	SNL G-205

A Note on Errors

Every effort that time and finance has afforded has been implemented to bring you a factual account of how The Sherman Tank looked in service during the Second World War.